Library and Information Science in a Digital Era

K.T. Dilli

ATLANTIC
PUBLISHERS & DISTRIBUTORS (P) LTD

Published by
ATLANTIC
PUBLISHERS & DISTRIBUTORS (P) LTD
7/22, Ansari Road, Darya Ganj,
New Delhi-110002
Phones : +91-11-23273880, 23275880, 23280451
Fax : +91-11-23285873
Web : www.atlanticbooks.com
E-mail : info@atlanticbooks.com

Branch Office
5, Nallathambi Street, Wallajah Road,
Chennai-600002
Phones : +91-44-64611085, 32413319
E-mail : chennai@atlanticbooks.com

Printed in India at Nice Printing Press, A-33/3A, Site-IV, Industrial Area, Sahibabad, Ghaziabad, U.P.

Preface

Library and Information Science in a Digital Era is intended to serve as a companion and handbook for library professionals in general, and the beginners who have opted for Bachelor in Library and Information Science (BLIS) or Master in Library and Information Science (MLIS), through distance mode in particular. The rudiments of library and information science have been explained in simple language and lucid style with suitable examples wherever necessary.

The topics have been carefully selected by taking into consideration the syllabi of various Indian universities offering library and information science courses. The subject matter of the book has been divided into 14 chapters. The first 10 chapters provide basic information about library and information science such as classification and cataloguing of books, information sources and services, development of libraries in India, library associations, etc. while the last four chapters have been devoted to Information Technology, digital library and management, e-collections and networking, etc. List of Acronyms and Abbreviations, and Glossary of Technical Terms have been given for easy understanding by the beginners of LIS course while Bibliography has been provided to facilitate further reading on the subject.

I am indebted to several individuals who have contributed directly or indirectly to this attempt. I am particularly grateful to my parents, teachers and well-wishers who contributed ideas and thoughts for this book. I am thankful to Rev. Fr. A. Muthumalai S.J., Principal, Loyola College, and Rev. Dr. Fr. S. Peter S.J., Secretary, Loyola College for their constant support. I am deeply appreciative of the library staff of Loyola College for assisting me in getting this book published.

I hope this book will be well received by the student community pursuing the library and information science course as well as library professionals.

K.T. Dilli

Contents

List of Acronyms and Abbreviations

AACR	-	Anglo-American Cataloguing Rules
AGRIS	-	Agricultural Information System
ALA	-	American Library Association
ASLIB	-	Association of Special Libraries and Information Bureau
BARC	-	Bhabha Atomic Research Centre
BIOSIS	-	Biosciences Information Service of Biological Abstracts
BNB	-	British National Bibliography
CAS	-	Current Awareness Service
CC	-	Colon Classification
CCC	-	Classified Catalogue Code
CLRI	-	Central Leather Research Institute
CORE	-	Computer Readable Catalogue
CSIR	-	Council of Scientific and Industrial Research
DESIDOC	-	Defence Scientific Documentation Centre
DRTC	-	Documentation Research and Training Centre
DST	-	Department of Science and Technology
FAO	-	Food and Agricultural Organization
FID	-	International Federation of Documentation
HCL	-	Hindustan Computers Limited
IASLIC	-	Indian Association of Special Libraries and Information Centres

ICAR	-	Indian Council of Agricultural Research
ICSSR	-	Indian Council of Social Science Research
ICSU	-	International Council of Scientific Unions
IFPRI	-	International Food Policy Research Institute
IFLA	-	International Federation of Library Association
ILA	-	Indian Library Association
ILO	-	International Labour Organization
INB	-	Indian National Bibliography
INFLIBNET	-	Information Library Network
INIS	-	International Nuclear Information System
INSDOC	-	Indian National Scientific Documentation Centre
ISBD	-	International Standard Bibliographic Description
ISBN	-	International Standard Book Number
ISI	-	Indian Standards Institution/Indian Statistical Institute
ISIS	-	Indian Standards Information System
ISRO	-	Indian Space Research Organization
ISSN	-	International Standard Serial Number
KWAC	-	Key Word And Conteset
KWIC	-	Key Word In Conteset
KWOC	-	Key Word Out of Conteset
MARC	-	Machine Readable Catalogue
MEDLARS	-	Medical Literature Analysis and Retrieval System
MEDLINE	-	Medlars on Line
NIC	-	National Information Centre
NICNET	-	National Informatics Centre Network
NISSAT	-	National Information System for Science and Technology
POPSI	-	Postulate Based Permuted Subject Indexing

PRECIS	-	Preserved Context Indexing System
R&D	-	Research and Development
ROM	-	Read Only Memory
RRC	-	Reactor Research Centre
RUC	-	Regional Union Catalogue
SDI	-	Selective Dissemination of Information
SENDOC	-	Small Enterprises Centre
SERC	-	Structural Engineering Research Centre
TIFR	-	Tata Institute of Fundamental Research
UDC	-	Universal Decimal Classification
UGC	-	University Grants Commission
UNESCO	-	United Nations Educational Scientific and Cultural Organization
UNIMARC	-	UNIVERSAL MARC
UNISIST	-	United Nations International Science Information on Science and Technology

Concept of Library Science

1

Libraries provide the incentive to the development of educational, social and cultural activities. According to Dr. S.R. Ranganathan, the father of Library Science in India, "Libraries are not mere storehouses, they are rich springs from which knowledge flows out to irrigate the wide field of education and culture."

According to UNESCO's Terminology of Documentation, "Library is an organised collection of printed books and periodicals or of any other graphic or audio-visual materials and the service of a staff to provide and facilitate the use of such materials as are required to meet the informational, research, educational or recreational needs of its users."

The word 'Library' comes from the Latin word, 'Libraria', which means a place where books and other writings are kept. But the library of today is much more than a building stocked with books. It is a workshop for the students to accumulate knowledge and wisdom. Through its doors, everybody can step into a world of adventure. It is sometimes called a 'treasure-house with an open door'.

The library is a trinity of documents, users/readers and staffs.

The old concept of the library, i.e. "storehouse of recorded documents" has been replaced by the modern concept and it is now known as "information centre".

The modern library is expected to provide the following services to the users:

(a) Provide information services.
(b) Provide better reference services.
(c) Acquire, organize and put to use the reading material.
(d) Facilitate dissemination and retrieval of knowledge.
(e) Provide inter-library loan.
(f) Provide documentation services.
(g) Provide and enhance service by adopting mechanized and automated procedures (computers).

J.H. Herald suggested '5 Rs' for better information services. They are:

1. *right information* would go to
2. *right man* in the
3. *right amount* at the
4. *right time* and in the
5. *right form.*

To achieve the objectives of modern libraries, it is important to adopt the following principles:

(a) Organization
(b) Administration
(c) Cataloguing
(d) Classification
(e) Technical services such as circulation, acquisition, reference service, information retrieval, automation, etc.

We are living in an age of 'explosions'. The explosion which reigns supreme is the 'knowledge explosion'. According to J.S. Sharma, the following are the driving forces which have given birth to this explosion:

1. Progress made by science and technology during the last 150 years.
2. The democratization of political institutions throughout the world.
3. The popularization of education in all sections and society.
4. Introduction of communication systems.

5. Impact of Russian Revolution (1917), two world wars, emergence of nationalism, improvement of printing technology.
6. Establishment of the UNO and its specialised agencies including UNESCO.

Five Laws of Library Science

Dr. S.R. Ranganathan in 1928, formulated the fundamental laws of Library science on the basis of his rich experience and observations which he had in Europe and other countries. In 1931, in his book "Five Laws of Library Science", he enunciated the five laws of Library science, which are also fondly known as 'punch sheel' of Library science. They are:

1. Books are for use.
2. Every reader his or her book.
3. Every book its reader.
4. Save the time of the reader.
5. Library is a growing organism.

Later, Ranganathan revised these laws as follows:

1. Documents are for use.
2. Every reader his or her document.
3. Every document its reader.
4. Save the time of the reader (as well as of staff).
5. A Library is a growing organism.

While referring about the five laws Dr. S.R. Ranganathan said, "These form the normative principles which contain in a lateral form, all the library practices current at any time and to be evolved at a latter time." These five laws are called *normative principles* by Ranganathan. They are the very essence of library science, since they provide the basic concept and branches of Library science like, cataloguing, classification, technical services, organization and administration.

Books are for use

Dr. S.R. Ranganathan, in his first law, "Books are for use", lays emphasis on the word 'use' and stresses that the books should be used by the readers. It is true that in the bygone days books were merely 'preserved', since they were rare and handwritten. He vehemently attacks the old concept of library, i.e. the library is the storehouse of books kept under lock and key. As the printing press was invented books have been produced in large numbers and the old concept has gradually been given away.

The first law has revolutionised the old concept of libraries as mere conservator of books into libraries providing books for one and all. It should serve the community for which it exists. The following are the implications of the first law:

(a) The location of the library must be such that it is easily reachable by the users (in a suitable centre).

(b) The rules and regulations must be inviting.

(c) The library hours should be convenient to the users so that they are able to make the most use of the library.

(d) A careful selection of books must be made by the librarian in accordance to the interests of the readers.

(e) Financial position must be sound, since the free flow of men and material is a must.

(f) Proper library staff must be selected to assist and guide the users.

(g) Provision of reasonable comfort and suitable furniture to readers must be made.

Every reader his or her book

The second law, 'Every reader his or her book' follows the first law. The first law replaces the old concept 'books are for preservation', by 'books are for use'. The second law widens this concept still further, i.e. 'books are for all'. It takes into consideration the basic educational approach, which is, education for everybody without exclusion of any community, sex, caste, colour or creed.

The second law has thrown open the use of books to men, and women, young and old, city and country people, normal and abnormal. It provides books for the sick. In fact, it has democratised the library service to all. The following are the implications of the second law:

(a) Proper library legislations must be passed to provide public libraries to the general public.
(b) To have better services for the users, the library should provide inter-library loan facilities.
(c) The collection building should be in terms of the choice of the readers and not on the mere size of the collection.

Every book its reader

The third law, 'Every book its reader' relates to the finding out a reader for every book in the library. Whereas the second law envisaged the procuring of appropriate books for all, the third law revolutionises the process still further by finding out a reader for all books in the library. Hence, it is the duty of the Librarian to ease out the process of finding right book at the right time by providing good system of cataloguing, classification and shelf arrangement. The following are the implications of the third law:

(a) To provide open access system to enable the readers to find books by themselves.
(b) To provide easy ways to find the books, like classification, cataloguing and arrangement.
(c) To provide good books at the least cost (proper selection of books).
(d) To arrange books exhibitions, lectures, display, newsletter and bulletin (extension service).

Save the time of the reader

The fourth law, 'Save the time of the reader' stresses the importance of time saving devices like open access, easy location and simplified issue-return system. The following methods may be taken into consideration to achieve the objectives of the fourth law:

(a) Proper reference service must be made available.
(b) Follow open access system.
(c) Provide stack room guides (bay guides) for each section.

(d) Provide card system, instead of register, at the counter.

(e) Cataloguing and classification system should be simplified.

(f) Provide documentation services like photocopying and translation.

(g) Provide guide cards (analytical entries, 'see' and 'see also' cross reference entries).

Library is a growing organism

The fifth law, 'Library is a growing organism' emphasises the importance of planning, organization and functions of the library. This law stresses the biological fact that only a growing organism will survive and an organism which ceases to grow shall perish. The modern library is a trinity of three factors, namely, book-reader-staff. In course of time new books are added, readers increase and new staff is employed. Thus library grows in stature and the librarian must plan everything taking into consideration the above. This law should be kept in mind even while constructing the library building.

Hence, proper planning at the initial stage should be done to meet the eventuality without any disruption. The following are the implications of this law:

(a) Cataloguing entries must be prepared taking into consideration the future growth.

(b) Provision of expansion should be there in every aspect—book, finance, furniture and other facilities.

(c) As a growing organism also replaces old and worn out parts, weeding out books must be a regular feature.

(d) To preserve books, procedures like rebinding, lamination, etc. must be followed.

(e) The classification scheme must be comprehensive, capable of addition and expansible.

These five fundamental laws of Dr. S.R. Ranganathan, constitute the very basis of library science.

Development of Libraries in Indian Context

2

The libraries have been in existence from the beginning of the civilisation or better still from the time when man learnt the art of recording and communicating ideas. Development of libraries is related to the educational, cultural and industrial development of a nation. Libraries are the life line for research and academic scholarship and spread of literacy and formal education.

India has now the third largest higher educational network in the world. Enrolment in higher education accounts for 40 per cent of the enrolment in the developing countries. Every eighth student enrolled in higher education on the globe is an Indian. Currently, over 2,50,000 teachers are engaged in the system. There are about 184 universities, 16,885 colleges and over 4 million students in India today.

According to C.D. Sharma, "Library service is a social and intellectual phenomenon which depends upon the awareness of the people regarding the utility of library services. Factors like the educated and awakened masses, industrial development and cultural hunger create social pressure for the changing dimensions of libraries and their services in any country."

The pioneer of library movement in India, Sayajirao Gaekwad said, "A library is instituted to preserve the records of the deeds and thoughts of men, for the instruction and enlightenment of future generations, so that those who are about to take up their share of the work of the world, their own part in the advance of the human race in intelligence, in civilization, in power, may start using the achievements by the countless generations before them."

Early Libraries

In ancient times knowledge was disseminated only orally. People believed in hearing and remembering as two effective modes of learning. The development of libraries and the spread of knowledge through recorded communication has always been interlinked. Whether it was Brahmanical or Buddhist, the Jain or Islamic system, the usual practice was communication by word of mouth and learning by rote through repetition of spoken words.

The production of literary works in the form of manuscripts was there even in the days of Panini. In the epic age, manuscript reading was prevalent in spite of patronage to oral teaching. In ancient India, the teachers were the moving repositories of knowledge. They could memorise and recite or reproduce a large number of works, immediately from memory. On the basis of their learning, observation and experience, they created new works. When it came to writing, the materials used for recording knowledge were copperplates, palm leaves, brick bark, cloth, wood, etc. Writing of books by hand, copying and recopying took much time and labour. Hence, books and consequently, libraries were not so common.

The libraries of ancient India are probably as old as Indus Valley civilization. In ancient India, libraries were known as *granthghar, pustakalaya*, etc. in which a large number of cylindrical seals and tablets with some inscriptions on them were stocked. No specific evidence throwing light on the organization, administration and the nature of the holdings of these libraries is available.

From the accounts of Fa-Hien and Hiuen-Tsang, the Chinese travellers, it is clear that writing and copying of texts was not unknown in India during the 5th century A.D. From their accounts, it is clear that monastic libraries were in vogue in that period. The libraries attached to important centres of learning in Eastern and Central India were Nalanda, Odantapuri, Vikramshila, Somapuri, Jaggadal and Mithila.

Nalanda, the university and a famous Buddhist centre was maintaining a splendid library to meet the needs of the numerous teachers and students. Nalanda University possessed a rich collection, both Buddhistic and non-Buddhistic. Nalanda was at the peak of its reputation and international glory in the 9th century A.D. The magnificent library and university were destroyed towards the end of the 12th century by the Muslim invaders.

With the advent of the Moghuls in India, libraries, along with other institutions of social and cultural life received considerable impetus. With the emergence of Babar rule in India, the Imperial Library was established for the use of Emperor as well as the nobles and scholars of the court. New and rare additions were made to the Imperial Library in the reign of Akbar.

Modern Libraries

Modern European scholars associate the beginning of the modern age with the invention of printing using moveable typewriter by John Gutenberg of Germany in 1454. This invention brought about a great revolution in the world of books all over Europe and its effect was felt in various parts of the world. With the invention of printing, the history of library science entered a new phase.

The history of the library movement in modern India can be traced from the advent of Britishers into this country. It was the evangelical flavour of the Christian missionaries which prompted them to promote learning by introducing printing presses and establishment of libraries. During the 19th century, the public libraries were established with the active support of the Europeans at Calcutta, Madras and Bombay. The year 1808 was a landmark in the history of library movement, since the Bombay Government initiated a proposal to register libraries which would receive free copies of books published from the funds for the encouragement of literature.

One of the main causes for the development of libraries with the coming of the British was the introduction of English education which contributed to the transformation of India particularly in the latter half of the 19th century. The first five universities were founded at Calcutta, Bombay, Madras, Allahabad and Lahore.

In the history of education in India, the year 1854 is an important one, since in that year came out the famous Educational Despatch of Charles Wood. It recommended the government to create a properly articulated scheme of education from primary to university level. As a result, the Central Legislation in 1857, passed Acts for the establishment of universities at Calcutta, Bombay and Madras. In 1901, Calcutta Public Library was purchased by the Government (then named as Imperial Library and now called the National Library) and was thrown open to the public. The opening of the Imperial Library is a landmark in the history of libraries in India.

The credit for providing a network of state aided public libraries to the society at large, goes to the ruler of Baroda, Sri Sayajirao Gaekwad. He said, "There is no more enabling thing than the reading of good books; it leads men along flowery pathways towards earnest and pure lives. I would bring to the poor man or woman, the ordinary man of bazaar, the common people everywhere, this wealth of literature now only known to the educated."

Library Movement in India

The library movement in India, however, is said to have begun with the beginning of the 20th century. The first All India Library Conference was convened at Madras, in 1912. This resulted in the establishment of an association at national level by the name of 'All India Public Library Association' with its headquarters at Vijayawada. With the efforts of S.R. Ranganathan and K.V. Krishnaswami Aiyer, Madras Library Association (MALA) was started in 1928. Similarly, such library associations were started in Punjab (1929), Bihar (1936), Assam (1939) and Trivandrum (1945).

The outbreak of Second World War was characterised by the rapid spread of the idea of democracy and a desire to preserve its ideals. As a result of this, the role of library service in helping to create such citizenry was realised. It is in the same period, the Indian National Congress and other nationalist organizations passed resolutions for promoting libraries and reading rooms but, for want of funds and public support, only reading rooms could be established in many parts of the country.

After independence, the first Library Legislation in India, 'Madras Public Libraries' was enacted in 1948. It was followed by states like Andhra Pradesh, Karnataka, Maharashtra and West Bengal enacting library legislations. As a result of UNESCO's pilot project of Delhi Public Library and the Library Development plan—30-year programme of Delhi University, a number of Science laboratories, Scientific and Research Institutes were established in India.

The Government of India, in every Five-Year Plan, allocated a sizeable amount of money towards the establishment of new libraries and the development of existing libraries. In 1953, Ministry of Education appointed an Advisory Committee for libraries to survey the existing system and to suggest betterment. It is said to be the landmark in the development of libraries in India.

Library Legislation

The term 'legislation' is defined as, 'enactment of laws or the laws enacted by a legislative power'. Dr. S.R. Ranganathan defines legislation as "laying down of instructions to persons responsible for running the government in order to properly discharge each of its functions".

Library legislation is very important for the establishment, development and maintenance of public libraries in any state. It is true that the libraries today have become the media of mass education. They are the cultural centres of a society. To finance these important social institutions and make them more useful and effective in the service of humanity, library legislation is considered essential.

Planned library development was not possible in the past, since the library facilities were available to those who paid only and those who did not pay were denied of the facilities. Moreover, the libraries were run by charity and donation from the rich people.

Provision of better library service to the reading community needs sufficient funds. This can be done by levying a cess for the library service. In turn, the taxation paves way for the enactment of a law in the form of library legislation.

Uses of Library Legislation

The following are the uses of library legislation:

(a) It is the library legislation which makes provision for service to all people irrespective of caste, sex, colour and creed.

(b) It makes provision for free service to all people.

(c) It guarantees the continuous flow of financial aid for the maintenance of libraries.

(d) The legislation provides for a proper constitution of authorities who are answerable to the general public.

Realising the importance of the library legislation, many countries from East and West have enacted Public Libraries Act. In India, the first Public Library Act was enacted in 1948 in Madras. The credit of enacting the first Public Libraries Act goes to Dr. S.R. Ranganathan. It was followed by Hyderabad Public Libraries Act in 1955, Andhra Pradesh in 1960, Karnataka in 1965, Maharashtra in 1967, and West Bengal in 1979. Many states are on the verge of enacting Public Libraries Act.

Types of Libraries

Library is the repository of human knowledge. Different types of libraries have been established to cater to the needs of various communities such as the general public, academic research workers, businessmen, specialists, etc. In general, libraries can be divided into three types. They are:

1. Public Libraries
2. Academic Libraries
3. Special Libraries.

Public Library

The public library is often called the 'People's University' for its universal character. The public library is an institution for the people, of the people, by the people. It is—for all, without the distinction of caste, creed, class, colour or sex.

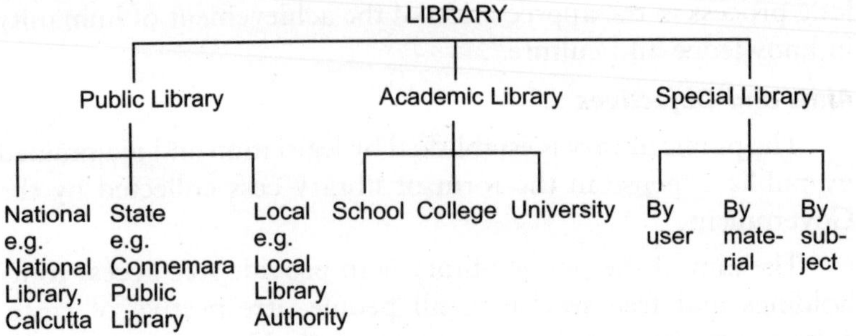

According to UNESCO's 'Terminology of Documentation', public library is "a library which serves the population of a community or region free of charge or for a nominal fee".

According to R.N. Chopra, "the public library refers to a library which is approved wholly or partly from public funds, and the use of which is not restricted to any class of persons in the community but is freely available to all".

Dr. S.R. Ranganathan compares the public library with academic library and says, "Academic Libraries can serve only a small fraction of the community. The rest must depend for their life-long self-education on a second species of libraries in the national network—the public library. It has the advantage over academic libraries in that the benefit it can bestow is global; the public library is a source not merely of information but also of recreation and inspiration." He further explains the term public library as, "the word 'public' denotes, in the first place, that such libraries are maintained at public expense—out of local rates and the state taxes. Since their benefits accrue to the community as a whole, the community supports them. It also denotes that their service is free to the public: they levy no subscriptions or fees."

UNESCO's public library manifesto proclaims: "Public library is a living force for education, culture and information and is an essential agent for the fostering of peace and understanding between people and between nations." It further says that "the public library is a practical demonstration of democracy's faith in universal education as a continuing and life long process in the appreciation of the achievement of humanity in knowledge and culture".

Aims and Objectives

The public library is established by legislation and maintained by public expense in the form of library cess collected by the Government.

The aim of the public library is to provide free access to its holdings and free service to all people, irrespective of caste, colour, sex, creed, rich, poor, young and old.

The following are the objectives of a public library:

1. To contribute to sustaining the quality of life in all its aspects—educational, economic, industrial, scientific and cultural.
2. To promote the concept of a democratic society in which equal opportunities exist for all to develop into true citizens.
3. To promote and foster the free flow of information and ideas.
4. To assist formal, adult and self-education.
5. To create and promote reading habit.

Functions

The public library has to function in such a way as to fulfil the above objectives. The following are the essential functions of the public libraries:

1. Education
2. Information
3. Culture
4. Leisure/recreation
5. To act as an extension agency by cultural festivals, lectures, film shows, etc.

Public Libraries in India

The public library is a product of modern democracy and by its nature and scope it is a library for every citizen. Hence, the clientele includes people from all walks of life who are literate, neo-literate or illiterate.

The public libraries in India may be categorised as:

(a) National

(b) State Government

(c) Local Bodies.

After independence, many states have established State Central Libraries and District Library Systems which are working well and providing book service to all. Among prominent states are Andhra Pradesh, Maharashtra and Karnataka.

In 1950, Delhi Public Library was established. It was one of the significant events in the development of public libraries in India. It was a pilot project co-sponsored by UNESCO and the Ministry of Education, Government of India.

(a) *National Library*. For any country, a National Library is like a living monument representing culture and glory of the nation. It is the only institution capable of preserving for the future the whole of each country's output and ensuring that bibliographical work proceeds on uniform lines. In India, the Imperial Library at Calcutta was redesignated as National Library of India in 1948. The National Library has the following objectives:

1. To act as a chief depository of all printed documents of that country.
2. Responsible for the compilation and the publication of National Bibliography.
3. To act as a centre for the whole country's library system by providing all assistance within and outside the country.
4. To act as the reservoir of the nation's literary output (entire holdings) by providing current, retrospective and foreign literature.

Hence a national library is a library commanding national character both in the matter of organization of resources and uses.

In order to promote public libraries in India, the Government of India enacted the Delivery of Books (public libraries) and Newspapers Act, 1954. In accordance to this Act, four copies of books and other publications brought out in India must be sent to the following libraries within a month of their publication:

1. National Library (Calcutta),
2. Central Library (Bombay),
3. Connemara Public Library (Madras), and
4. Delhi Public Library (Delhi).

(b) *State Government Libraries*. After independence, many states have established State Central Libraries and District Libraries. A State Central Library also functions as a local library for the city where it is situated—many of these libraries have branch libraries, mobile libraries and children's libraries. These libraries provide reference and lending facilities to all people. Their collections are such that they can serve the informational needs of the highly educated as well as the neo-literates.

(c) *Local Bodies Libraries*. The Local Body Libraries are normally run by private individuals and organizations, such as, Nagri Pracharni Sabha, Varanasi; Hardinge Public Library, Delhi; Acharya Narendra Dev Library, Lucknow. These libraries mostly depend upon endowments, gifts and donations. Most of them charge subscription from the users. At many places where the government run public libraries are either inadequate or are not available, these libraries greatly help to meet the requirements of the people.

Academic Library

The academic libraries are the next most important libraries which include:

(a) School,
(b) College, and
(c) University libraries.

Any library attached to the above institutions is known as an academic library. The academic library differs in purpose, scope and service from a public library and a special library. The main objective of the academic library is to function as an auxiliary of the institution in which it exists. Its main function is to serve the needs of students and faculties in formal institutions. It is generally believed that an institution is judged by its library.

According to Prof. S. Gupta, "The quality of the academic library, that is, the school library, the college library and the university library, is conditioned not wholly, but largely, by the quality of education the academic institution imparts, which in turn depends directly on the quality of its teachers, their teaching methods, the policy of educational administration, and indirectly, on the Government which has to find money for the general improvement of such academic institutions." The Education Commission under the chairmanship of Kothari stressed the important role of libraries in academic institutions in imparting better education.

(a) *School Library*. Psychologically it is a child who is always curious to know many things than the grown-ups. With this curiosity, the child comes to the school. Hence it is the duty of the school authorities to provide suitable atmosphère for the all-round development of the child. The child will not be satisfied unless it is fed with facts and figures. Undoubtedly the school library can undertake the responsibility of serving the curiosity of the child.

It is believed that the books that a child reads, in addition to the textbooks, shape his character and determine his ideal for the future.

The school library should create the reading habit among children. This will, in turn, help them to make the best use of college, university and public libraries in future. The collection in a school library must include junior reference sources, books supplementing the prescribed reading materials. The main objective of the school library is to create reading habits among the children.

(b) *College Library*. As college library is an important and integral part of the teaching programme, it occupies a prominent position. The present day college education has become student centred and it encourages students to play a vital and creative role in their own education. The college library is one of the means to achieve their ends. The aims of college education and college libraries are interrelated. The college library provides ample opportunities for self-education to the students, besides supplementing the class lectures.

Realising the important role of the college libraries, the UGC has been granting special sums of money towards the development of college libraries. The following are the objectives of a college library:

1. To provide suitable supplementary books to assist students and faculties.
2. To provide necessary information on how to tap suitable information.
3. To encourage students to face the world with confidence.
4. To provide assistance for self-education by providing suitable documents to students.
5. To assist teaching faculties in organising the syllabi and methods of teaching.
6. To provide important assistance like the latest developments in various fields of the teaching staff.

(c) *University Library*. University library is primarily concerned with the conservation and propagation of basic knowledge and ideas as well as their research and interpretation activities.

Dr. Radhakrishnan in "University Education Commission Report" defined a library as 'the heart of a university's work'. In other words, both for humanities and scientific research, a well organized library is essential in a university.

For higher education the university is the centre of learning and the centre of intellectual activity. Hence, the duty of the university librarian is to help in the dissemination and advancement of knowledge. The university library is not only a storehouse of books, but it is a dynamic agency to assist the scholars and researchers in carrying on their pursuits in the advancement of knowledge by making use of the library books extensively. The aims, as defined by Radhakrishnan's report are the "dissemination of learning and search for new knowledge". The aim of university education should be the aim of a university library.

The university library is expected to cater to the varied needs of graduates, postgraduates, research scholars and faculty members. Normally, the collection of university library consists of books related to their curriculum, supplementary reading and books for teaching and research. Besides, the library has to subscribe to many current useful journals related to the research scholars and has to possess non-book materials such as microfilms and microfiche.

We can sum up the objectives of university library as:

1. To support the university's total programme.
2. To supply more specialised service to those who seek information in the specific field of study.
3. To arrange essential reading materials and other library facilities for the smooth running of all formal programmes of learning.
4. To keep the faculty members informed of the latest thoughts in their respective fields.
5. To guide research scholars and provide them the resources useful to enhance the research projects.

The first phase of the development of higher education took place when Charles Wood shaped a plan for higher education and three universities of Calcutta, Bombay and Madras were established in presidency towns in 1857. Calcutta University was the first among them which established its library in a collection received by way of donation.

With a view to improve the standards of university libraries, several committees were formed and they duly emphasized the importance of university libraries. One of its recommendations was the establishment of University Grants Commission, which has been directly responsible for assisting financially to the development of university libraries. Since its establishment in 1956, the UGC has been providing all possible assistance to the universities.

Special Libraries

The Special Library is the product of the 20th century. It is directly related to scientific and technological research and industrial development.

A library which is devoted for a specialised activity such as for the requirements of specialists or of some special institutions is known as special library.

A special library, in other words, is devoted to various specific disciplines and subjects. It is for special groups and various specific organizations.

Need for Special Libraries

The following are the chief factors which gave rise to special libraries:

(a) Explosion of information, in other words, the tremendous growth of specialised literature (books, periodicals and other materials).

(b) Necessity to provide some specific piece of information to specific readers (approach to specific information).

(c) Application of the results of research for further growth of subject areas.

It is generally believed that the general libraries may not be able to satisfy the specific needs of the special type of information seekers who are in the Research and Development wing (R&D). Hence the need for establishment of special libraries for a specific field. The following are the special libraries established in India:

1. Birla Institute of Technology.
2. Council of Scientific and Industrial Research (CSIR).
3. Indian Institute of Science.
4. Indian Statistical Institute.
5. Institution of Mathematical Science.
6. National Chemical Research Laboratory.
7. Botanical Survey of India.
8. Zoological Museum Library.

9. Indian Council of Agricultural Research (ICAR).
10. Central Leather Research Institute (CLRI).

Objectives

The basic objective of the special library is to provide latest information to those who are engaged in promoting the interests of the organization. Since the users of the special libraries are definite in their purpose and need exact and accurate information, these libraries are expected to provide exact latest information at the right time. Hence the special libraries exist to provide facts and information rather than recreation and leisure.

The collection of a special library may contain latest edition of books and current journals of the specific field, press releases, reports, working papers, archival material, directories, etc.

The special library is expected to provide the following services to the special users:

1. To provide photocopying facilities.
2. To provide Selective Dissemination of Information (SDI).
3. To provide documentation services like translation, indexing and abstracting.
4. To provide on-line system through computer terminals.
5. To provide bibliographic services.
6. To provide inter-library loan facilities.

The special libraries are located in different kinds of institutions, organizations and enterprises. The collections of special libraries are generally limited to specific subjects or groups of allied subjects. Special libraries may be categorised in the following three ways:

1. By user (Example, 'Prison Library').
2. By material (Example, 'Manuscript Library', Tanjore in Tamil Nadu).
3. By subject (Example, 'Central Leather Research Institute'—CLRI, Madras).

The organization which provides specialised library services has definite policies and commitments to a community. The users of these libraries are very purposeful and they make use of the resources of the library in pursuit of their objectives. These libraries provide facts and information rather than recreation. Supply of periodicals and bound volumes to users is one of the important services offered in the special library. If the required periodical is not available for reference in a library, the librarian has to make an effort to locate the same in another library and procure it on inter-library loan.

Library as an Information Centre

3

Information

According to UNISIST, information is, "a sensible statement, opinion, fact, concept or idea, or an association of statements, opinions or ideas. It is closely associated with knowledge, in that, once information has been assimilated, correlated and understood, it becomes knowledge."

In other words information may be defined as 'the data placed into a meaningful context for its recipients'.

In the words of Eliahu Hoffman, "Information is an aggregate (collection or accumulation) of statements, or facts or figures which are conceptually, by way of reasoning, logic, idea, or any other mental 'mode of operation', interrelated."

As information is a processed data in a meaningful form, it can be tapped from different sources. The Sources of Information chart is shown on next page.

Information Service

The Scientific Renaissance of 16th century and the Industrial Revolution led to enormous growth of reading materials. As a result, the researchers found it difficult to cope with this huge volume of materials. In order to solve the problem of information explosion, the information service was started in scientific and technical libraries.

The information service has been defined as "service provided by, or for any information centre which can be of interest to potential users of the service". This is done by preparing and

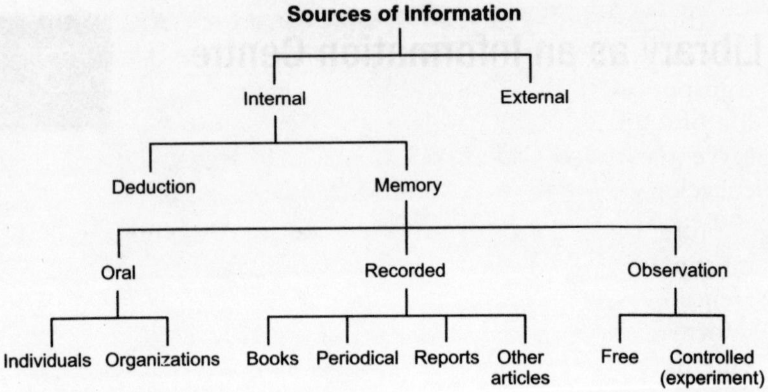

circulating news letters, literature surveys, reading lists, abstracts or articles in current periodicals, etc.

Types

The modern library is expected to serve information in two aspects:

(a) provision of information on demand.

(b) provision of information in anticipation.

In the former, the user approaches the reference librarian with a specific requirement of information and he is served with necessary information on demand. Whereas in the latter, the user is well informed of the latest and up-to-date information; in other words, the user is kept abreast of the latest information.

Melvin Voight has identified four types of information needs or approaches. They are:

(a) Current approach,

(b) Everyday approach,

(c) Exhaustive approach, and

(d) Catching-up approach.

(a) *Current approach*. The users involved especially in research and development require nascent or the latest information on some factual problem, e.g. the percentage of population of a country, literacy percentage, etc. The reference librarian may supply the information by making use of year books, Government documents, etc.

(b) *Everyday approach.* In this category, the users require specific information like information on the means of transportation and communication; meaning of a scientific term, life of a great scientist and so on. The reference librarian may serve these users by making use of reference sources like encyclopaedia and world bibliography.

(c) *Exhaustive approach.* Here the users require specialized information which may or may not be available in the library. Hence the reference librarian has to seek other libraries for information to serve these potential users. It may require some time to satisfy the clientele. Time is involved in this category, since the librarian has to get the documents on inter-library loan.

(d) *Catching-up approach.* In general the users are quite often faced with the problem of what to read. In this situation the reference librarian assists the users in meeting their informational needs. He provides information especially about the new arrivals and useful books on a subject of their specialisation.

One of the basic aims of information service is "putting the knowledge to work". The modern library is established with the responsibility of organising and preserving the recorded human thoughts to achieve its basic objective of dissemination of information.

The following information services have become necessary with the exponential growth of literature which includes books, periodicals, serials and other micro documents:

1. Information retrieval services like SDI and CAS. (Selective Dissemination of Information & Current Awareness Service.)
2. Documentation services like photocopying, translation, indexing and abstracting.
3. Bibliographic services.
4. Paper clipping services for the current information contained in newspapers.
5. Inter-library loan services.

The modern library is an information centre, since it involves preserving, organising and disseminating the information for the benefit of the users in general and the society in particular. In other words, the modern library does the work of an information centre by providing the right information at the right moment to the right person in the right way.

Information Centre

The primary aim of information service is 'putting the knowledge to work'. The primitive civilised men preserved knowledge in clay tablets, stones, inscriptions in caves, etc. But the modern man preserves knowledge in books, microfiche, audio and video cassettes and macro chips.

The Industrial Revolution paved the way for research activities. As a result, knowledge exploded and this resulted in documents explosion. The proliferation of literature in scientific area resulted in the research and scientific personnel facing the following problems:

1. It became difficult for them to judge how many documents would be useful.
2. They were faced with financial constraints.
3. They had to waste time in getting the right information from the heap of documents.
4. Delay in getting the piece of information.

The above-mentioned problems directly helped in establishing information centres to cater to the needs of researchers and scientists.

The following eight functions were identified for an information centre:

1. Collection of data
2. Selection of data
3. Classifying
4. Arranging
5. Storing
6. Retrieving
7. Documentation (reproduction)
8. Dissemination.

Library as an Information Centre

Library, in modern days, is regarded as a social institution. To cater to the different needs of the readers, different libraries have been established like public libraries, academic libraries, and special libraries.

Realising the importance of libraries as information centres, public and private organizations have established different libraries.

Functions

The following are the functions of a library as an information centre:

1. Collection of documents/materials.
2. Processing of documents/materials.
3. Storage of information.
4. Retrieval of information.
5. Dissemination of information.
6. Evaluation of information.

If we compare the functions of an information centre with that of a library, it would be clear that library functions as an information centre.

Library Associations

4

Library Associations

The term 'Library Association' is used for the association responsible for the examination and certification of library workers, the accumulation and dissemination of general information concerning libraries and the establishment and propagation of general standards in librarianship.

In other words, the 'Library Association' is 'a body of persons associated for a common purpose'. It is essential for the profession to be well-organized to make it effective in the service of its members. In order to fulfil the above purpose, the librarians, especially of the United States of America and the United Kingdom established National Library Associations in their respective lands as early as in 1875 and 1877, respectively. Other countries slowly followed and established their National Library Associations. It is estimated that at least 300 library associations throughout the world, are functioning currently.

National Library Associations

It was Melvil Dewey, who was responsible for the organization of the first American Library Association in 1876. It was the first National Library Association in the world. It was followed by the British Library Association of U.K. By the tireless efforts of eminent librarians in India, the Indian Library Association (ILA) was organised in 1933.

American Library Association (ALA)

The American Library Association was the first national association in the world. It was organised by Melvil Dewey in

1876. Its main aim was to promote the libraries and the librarians to serve the society better by providing professional standards for the librarians.

The motto of the 'American Library Association' is 'the best reading for the greatest number at the least cost'. The headquarters of the ALA is situated in Chicago.

The following are the duties and responsibilities of ALA in U.S.A.:

1. It promotes library legislation both at the national and the state level to improve the quality of library service in the country. In turn, it paves the way for the development of public libraries in rural areas.
2. It tries to inculcate the feeling that an American has the right to read anything he wants without any censorship.
3. It provides facilities to the libraries to select books.
4. It promotes library education and puts forth standards for library schools in the U.S.A.
5. It is responsible for the international relations in library affairs by working as a clearing house for information on international library affairs.
6. It fully cooperates with the international library bodies like IFLA, FID and UNESCO.
7. It is one of the members in bringing out the 'Anglo-American Cataloguing Rules' (AACR I & II).

British Library Association (BLA)

The British Library Association (BLA) was organised in 1877 with the motto 'the thoughts of men are common wealth'. The basic aim of BLA is to help all library professionals in establishing better standards and better library administration in their profession.

The following are the duties and responsibilities of the British Library Association (BLA):

1. To promote library registration and guide public libraries to conduct professional training programmes and examinations.

2. To conduct surveys of the existing public libraries of England. It also undertakes surveys of library services in Commonwealth countries under the title 'Libraries in the Commonwealth'.
3. It is responsible for improvement of the status and salaries of librarians.
4. It undertakes professional training programmes and examinations of librarians.
5. It provides assistance and encouragement in bringing out the British National Bibliography (BNB).
6. It cooperates with the international bodies like IFLA, FID and UNESCO and international organizations like British Council.
7. It conducts International Exhibition in cooperation with other National Associations.

Indian Library Association (ILA)

India has two Library Associations of national stature. One is the Indian Library Association (ILA) and the other is the Indian Association of Special Libraries and Information Centre (IASLIC).

As mentioned in Chapter 2 'Development of Libraries in Indian Context', the British education system and the invention of printing press had an impact on the Indian society. The result was the emergence of new class of literature and educated people and the demand for books and periodicals began to increase. This, in turn, resulted in establishment of more libraries. The librarians in India began to realise the importance of a national library association.

With the tireless efforts of eminent librarians, the 'Indian Library Association' (ILA) was founded on 12 September 1933, during the course of a conference which was inaugurated by J. Leitch Wilson, the then Educational Commissioner, Govt. of India. More eminent amongst the founder members of the association were K.M. Asadullah, S.R. Ranganathan, Kumar Munidra, Deb Rai Mahasaya and so on.

During the first thirteen years of its existence, seven annual conferences were held. Prominent amongst its activities during that period were:

1. The ALA drew up a scheme for the inter-library loan.
2. Compiled a Directory of Indian Libraries.
3. Drafted a Model Library Bill. Besides, it started the publication of a quarterly in 1942.

Objectives

The following are the objectives of the ILA:

1. Promotion and furtherance of the library movement in India.
2. Providing training facilities to librarians and facilitating research in library science.
3. Improving the service conditions, salaries and status of librarians.
4. Cooperating with international organizations and associations.
5. Supporting the policy of establishment of information and documentation centres.

Duties of ILA

1. ILA has been pressing the government for passing proper legislation for the rapid improvement of libraries in our country.
2. ILA has been pleading for the uniformity in the standards of library education in Indian universities.
3. ILA has also drafted a Model Library Bill for the benefit of the government.
4. ILA has been highlighting the social status of the librarians and striving for them better service conditions.
5. ILA celebrates National Library Day on 14th of November and National Library Week from 14th to 20th of November every year.

ILA cooperates with international organizations like 'International Federation of Library Associations and Institutions

(IFLA)' and 'Commonwealth Library Association (COMLA)'. ILA has to its credit the following publications both in English and Hindi:

1. Directory of Indian Libraries.
2. Union Catalogue of Periodical Holdings in the South Asian Libraries.
3. ILA Bulletin.
4. ILA Newsletter.
5. Library Bulletin (1942-46).

Though we have achieved many things through the ILA, but we have still some objectives yet to achieve, namely, the nationwide library legislation and nationwide network of public library system.

IASLIC

The IASLIC came into existence at the general meeting, held on 3rd September 1955, at the Indian Museum, Calcutta. The IASLIC's contribution to the library profession is unique, in the sense that even non-library staff such as scientists, educators and administrators, who guide the destinies of research institutions have been brought close to this profession.

The IASLIC has undoubtedly raised librarians' status and has given a new look to the library profession. The IASLIC publishes books and brings out a quarterly by the name of 'IASLIC Bulletin'. It also makes a thorough and extensive survey of scientific and research libraries in India. It has been conducting regularly language classes in German and Russian and operating documentary reproduction and translation services for its constituent organizations.

The IASLIC also cooperates with the international professional organizations like IFLA and FID.

International Library Associations

To guide the national organizations all over the world, international agencies of the United Nations, such as WHO, FAO, ICSU, UNESCO and ILO have come into being and are actively functioning.

To cope with the information explosion and the tremendous output of printed materials, documents and references, several international bodies have come into the picture. The following are such international bodies:

(a) Federation of International Documentation (FID).
(b) International Council of Scientific Unions (ICSU).
(c) International Federation of Library Associations (IFLA).
(d) United Nations Educational Scientific and Cultural Organization (UNESCO).
(e) United Nations International Science Information on Science and Technology (UNISIST).

Federation of International Documentation (FID)

In 1895, Paul Outlet and Henri LaFontaine founded, in Brussels, the 'Institute International de Bibliographic', which later became the 'International Federation for Documentation'.

Objectives

The following are the objectives of the Federation:

1. To bring together at the international level and to coordinate the activities of organizations and individuals concerned with or interested in documentation.
2. To develop the study and organization of documentation.
3. To create an international network of documentation.

Activities

The following are the activities of FID:

1. To exchange the experience in relation to documentation among national and other interested organizations.
2. To create a forum for discussion of problems relating to documentation.
3. To revise the Universal Decimal Classification (UDC).
4. To assist the study and research of documentation.
5. To publish R&D projects in documentation and librarianship and FID News Bulletin.

International Council of Scientific Unions (ICSU)

The ICSU was founded in 1931 in Paris. It is an international non-governmental scientific organization composed of 17 autonomous international scientific unions and more than 60 national members, i.e., institutions of science, research councils or similar scientific institutions.

Objectives

The following are the objectives of ICSU:

1. To encourage international scientific activity for the benefit of mankind.
2. To act as a forum for the exchange of ideas, communication of scientific information.
3. To assist in the development of standards in methodology, nomenclature and units.

Activities

1. To initiate, design and coordinate international scientific research programmes like International Geophysical Year (IGY).
2. To organise international conferences, symposia and meetings of experts in all parts of the world.
3. To coordinate collaborative research programmes in interdisciplinary areas—Antarctic, oceanic, space and water research.

In 1934, ICSU started establishing relations with the Organization for Intellectual Cooperation of the League of Nations, UNESCO and UNISIST. The ICSU brings out a quarterly ICSU Bulletin.

International Federation of Library Association (IFLA)

In the International Conference of librarians and book lovers in Prague in 1926, a proposal to set up an International Committee which would constitute of representatives of national library associations, was accepted. The name 'International Federation of Library Association' (IFLA) came into being in the 3rd conference held in Stockholm in 1930.

Objectives

1. To promote international understanding.
2. To promote cooperation, discussion, research and development in all fields of library activities, including bibliography and information services.
3. To assist and promote the education of personnel.

Activities

The IFLA takes part in all the activities relating to libraries and its allied activities. The following are the activities of IFLA:

1. To provide expert advice and technical assistance in the planning and development of library services.
2. To direct funds obtained from UNESCO into practical projects for the development of libraries and library organizations.
3. To provide encouragement and assistance to countries whose associations are not functioning and thereby encouraging those countries to take part in the international activities.
4. To give a more effective voice to developing countries.
5. To hold IFLA conferences in each region to boost library activities (IFLA Conference was held in New Delhi in 1992).
6. To maintain the Universal Bibliographic Control (UBC).
7. To assist Asia, Africa, Latin America and Caribbean countries through its special divisions called the 'Divisions of Regional Activities'.

The IFLA also cooperates with the international organizations like UNESCO, FID, the International Council of Archives (ICA) and the International Standard Organization (ISO).

The IFLA has a number of publications to its credit. A few important ones are:

1. IFLA Journal (quarterly).
2. IFLA Annual Proceedings of the Meetings.

3. ISBD (M): International Standard Bibliographic Description for Monographic publications.
4. ISBD (S): International Standard Bibliographic Description for Serials.

United Nations Educational Scientific and Cultural Organization (UNESCO)

UNESCO is a specialised agency of the United Nations. Established in 1946, it is one of the 14 bodies with recognized competence. The UNESCO entirely differs in its activities from other bodies.

Aim

The chief aim of UNESCO is to promote peace, human rights and international understanding. The aim of UNESCO is often alluded to a phrase which says that since wars begin in the minds of men, it is in the minds of men that the defences of peace must be constructed.

Objectives

The following are the objectives of UNESCO:

1. To encourage international intellectual cooperation.
2. To speed up development through operational assistance to its member states.
3. To promote peace among the human beings.
4. To assist its member states in the development of their documentation and library services.

Information Services

The UNESCO in its varied programmes assists its member states in the development of their documentation and library services. It assists by striving for:

1. Improvement in the public library services.
2. Improvement in the university and special libraries. It has been undertaking series of activities involving seminars, technical assistance missions, grants and publications.

3. Exchange; it has organised conventions on the international exchange of publications.
4. Compilation of bibliography; it has launched, in cooperation with IFLA, an ambitious project called 'Universal Bibliographic Control' (UBC).
5. Publication of 'Bulletin' for libraries. It is an important contribution of UNESCO to the enrichment of librarians' professional experience and an effective means of communication between colleagues the world over.
6. Creation of "Regional Book Promotion Centres"; through this, the shortage of suitable books in vernacular languages is solved. Four such Regional Book Promotion Centres were set-up to assist this programme. They are at Tokyo, Yaoundi, Cairo and Bagota.
7. Establishment of ISORID (International Information System on Research in Documentation). It was established in cooperation with FID to collect, organise, analyse and disseminate information on research activities.
8. The maintenance and diffusion of knowledge by protecting the world's inheritance of books, encouraging the exchange of information material and initiating international cooperative efforts to give the people of all countries access to the publications produced by any one of them.
9. Imparting professional training to librarians. UNESCO assists in the form of meetings of experts, arrangement of specialised courses, setting up of regional training centres like those in Dakar (Senegal) and schools of librarians and granting of fellowships.

United Nations International Science Information on Science and Technology (UNISIST)

UNISIST is one of the UNESCO's programmes for international cooperation. It was based on a joint study by

UNESCO and ICSU. It was set up as a continuing inter-governmental programme for international cooperation in scientific and technical information.

Activities of UNISIST

1. To act towards developing national or regional information policies and infrastructures.
2. To act towards the improvement and strengthening of institutional and normative components of information transfer.
3. To develop specialised human resources essential to the planning and operation of future information networks.
4. To provide reference manual for 'Machine Readable Bibliographic Descriptions'.
5. To provide guidelines for the establishment and development of the thesaurus.

Library Organization and Management

5

Like other sciences, Library Science too has its fundamentals. These fundamentals are essential for the successful operation of a library and to coordinate its programme of dissemination of knowledge to its patrons. The following are the fundamentals of Library Science:

1. Organization
2. Administration
3. Classification
4. Cataloguing
5. Technical services like:
   (a) Acquisition
   (b) Book Selection
   (c) Circulation
   (d) Documentation
   (e) Resource-sharing
   (f) Reference service
   (g) Automation

In the present day, library science is called Information Science and the modern library is re-designated as Information Centre. The traditional terms used formerly for library organization and administration, have been replaced by the term 'Library Management'.

Organization

Organization is nothing but an organised body, similar to a biological organism. It has the characteristics of an organism like growth, development and maintenance of equilibrium. Library is a non-profitable and service oriented organization with an objective to serve its users to increase their knowledge.

'Organization' is the formation of an effective machine, management of an effective executive; administration of an effective direction. Hence, organization is the machine of management in its achievement of the ends determined by administration.

According to L.M. Harrod, "Library organization is an act of organising, i.e. creating a systematic union of individuals in a body whose officials, agents and members work together for a common end." In other words, 'Organization creates the machine; administration runs it.'

Library organization can be said to include:

(a) Planning and construction of library building.

(b) Planning and procurement of library equipment and furniture.

(c) Appointment of staff and their duties.

(d) Organization of library materials and coordination of the work of various departments and sections.

Management

The term 'Management' is a complex phenomena and is considered a basic and significant process to guide an organization to achieve its objectives effectively.

The Encyclopaedic Dictionary of Business defines the term 'management' as, "the manner in which a business is operated. It consists of the operation, supervision and execution of management policies."

According to Ivan S. Banki, management is, "a collective term that refers to the system, its functions, process or office of planning, providing, coordinating, directing, evaluating and controlling all available efforts and resources of organization for the accomplishment of the objectives and policies which are designed and handled by the top executive of the organization".

The concept of management has been defined in several ways by different authors. It was Gulick and Urwick who coined an acronym for the functions of management as POSDCORB. The acronym POSDCORB stands for the following library functions:

P	-	Planning
O	-	Organising
S	-	Staffing
D	-	Directing
Co	-	Coordinating
R	-	Reporting
B	-	Budgeting

Library Building

Planning and construction of library building is one of the important organizational functions. The library building has to be designed keeping in view its functions. The chief principles of library building planning should be simplicity, efficiency, economy, flexibility, functional usefulness and the avoidance of monumentality.

According to Charles C. Soule, the construction of library building should be planned according to the kind of work to be done and the community to be served.

According to Dr. S.R. Ranganathan, the library is a growing organism. Hence, the library building has to be constructed to meet the future requirements. Ranganathan in his fifth law of library science, 'Library is a growing organism' stresses the importance of ventilation and light. According to him, the windows of the stack room and the reading room should be so placed and so designed that these rooms get plenty of natural light and do not need artificial light except at night. This provision automatically secures free ventilation and avoids sunlight penetrating directly since it directly affects both books and readers. By sunlight, readers are enervated, books are dried up and warped, and their lives shortened.

While planning the construction of library building, due consideration should be given to aesthetics also. According to Ranganathan, the library should be beautiful and everything possible should be done to produce an atmosphere of serenity, composure and loveliness.

The following are the principles which should be considered before planning a library building:

1. Suitable site must be selected for the library building.
2. It should be an independent building and provision for future expansion should be made.
3. Suitable provision should be made for work place for staff.
4. The building should have proper natural lighting, ventiliation and control of noise.
5. It should not have a complex architecture.
6. Interior arrangement should be planned before the exterior.
7. Proper plan should be made to provide accommodation for readers near the books they want to use.
8. The building should have functional design rather than monumental.
9. There should be no trees very near the proposed library building.
10. Proper amenities like water and toilets should be provided and fire protection must be made.

The building committee must comprise of the following persons:

(a) Architect
(b) Librarian
(c) Library consultant
(d) Interior decorator
(e) Head of the Institution.

The librarian and the architect are directly concerned with the creation of library building. So they should be aware and

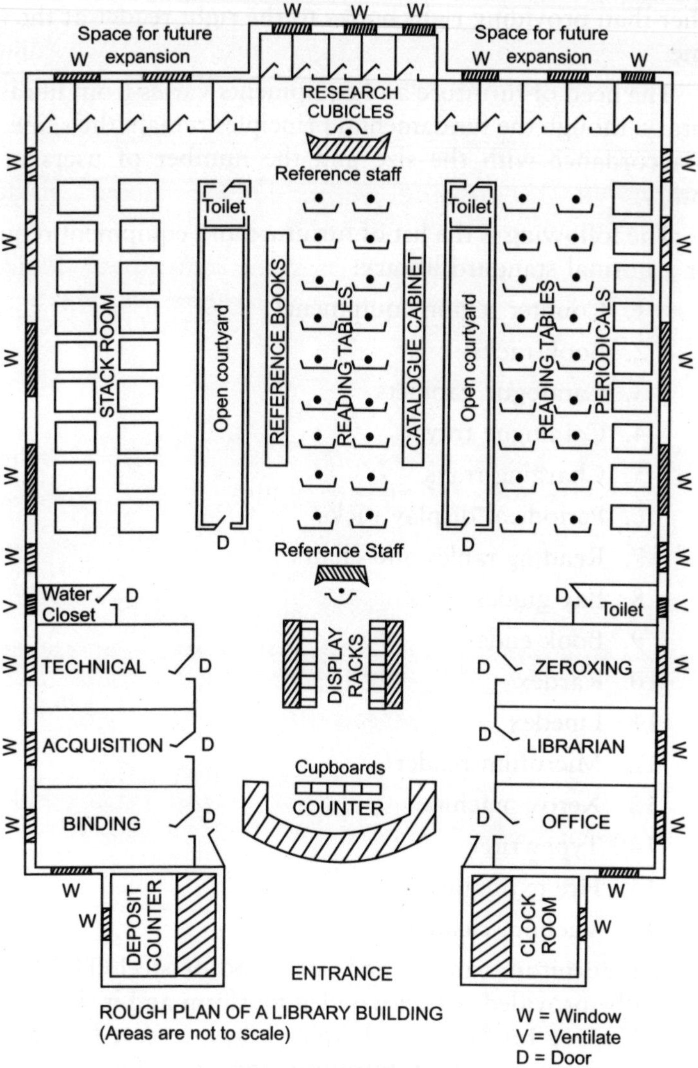

Fig. Library Building

well-versed in the above facts before construction of a library building.

Furniture and Equipment

The next most important thing is furniture and equipment. Proper facilities like furniture must be provided to the readers other than providing right books to the right reader at the right time.

The need of furniture and equipments varies from library to library, though the fundamental principles remain the same. It is in accordance with the size and the number of users of the library.

The following is the list of furniture and equipment required for a normal standard library:

1. Counter region equipments
2. Book racks
3. Catalogue cabinets
4. Catalogue trays
5. Charging trays
6. Periodical display racks
7. Reading tables and chairs
8. Bay guides
9. Book ends
10. Kardex
11. Linedex
12. Microfilm reader
13. Xerox machine
14. Typewriter
15. Fire extinguisher
16. Vacuum cleaner.

The furniture can be made of wood or steel. The counter should be provided with a wooden platform and it should have enough space for keeping charging trays, reserved books and reader's tickets. Built-in furniture and equipment should be avoided and the equipment to be purchased must have the quality of durability. Economy and ease of maintenance, simplicity, also comfort and convenience are important considerations. It is generally accepted among the librarians that while planning for construction of a new library building, the interior arrangement must be planned before the exterior.

Book Selection

It is a general notion that the importance of a library depends upon the reading material it contains and how efficiently that material is served to the users. A library is judged not by the volume it possesses but by the variety and quality of the books. In other words, 'books selection' is the rock on which library service is built.

Aim

The aim of book selection should be to build a collection which is dynamic and capable of meeting the changing needs and demands of the present and the future. The ultimate aim of book selection is to make the most effective use of the allotted book fund.

A library can neither possibly to acquire all the published material nor every thing published will be found useful in a library. Hence, proper selection of reading material is necessary. The book selectors should consider the following points while selecting books for the library. They are:

1. resources available,
2. users,
3. the area of coverage, and
4. avoiding multiple copies (duplication).

Book selection is one of the most important activities with which librarianship is concerned, for it is the stock of books which gives a library its character. The term is generally understood to mean the selection of books for addition to stock, but frequently the practicing librarian is required to choose books for other purposes such as select bibliographies, reading lists, displays, etc.

Theories of Book Selection

The eminent persons in librarianship have propounded various theories in connection with book selection. Among them the following three theories are found most useful and important. They are:

1. Dewey's motto—"The best reading for the largest number at the least cost."

2. McColvin's Demand Theory—"Demand for books should be differentiated according to its value, variety and volume."
3. Drury's Principle—"The high purpose of book selection is to provide the right book to the right reader at the right-time."

Selection Policy

The responsibility of book selection falls on the following persons:

1. Librarian
2. The Library Committee
3. Faculty

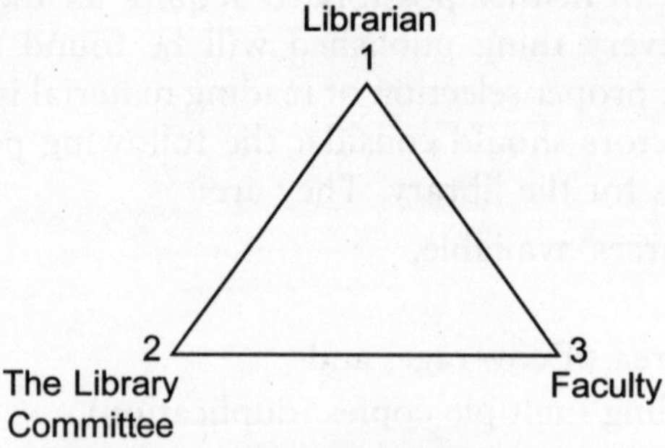

Book Selection

According to Boxler, book selection policy should be dependend upon the following factors:

1. Size of the institution,
2. Nature of curriculum, and
3. Funds.

It was Randall who analysed four categories of reading material. They are:

1. Reference material
2. Curricula material
3. General material
4. Research material.

It is the duty of the librarian to provide a well balanced collection having in mind the type of users and the availability of funds.

Sources for Book Selection

The librarian in his efforts to provide best books for the largest number at the least cost, has to rely on the following sources in selecting books:

1. Human sources.
2. Documentary sources.

The human sources comprise the following:

(a) Subject specialists.
(b) Heads of the departments.
(c) Research scholars.
(d) Library users.

The documentary sources include trade lists, bibliographies, secondary periodicals, Government publications and syllabi of various courses.

Tools

The following are the tools for book selection:

1. Bibliographies
   (a) Trade bibliographies (Books in print)
   (b) Subject bibliographies
   (c) National bibliographies (INB, BNB)
2. Book reviews
3. Book on approval
4. Book ordering.

The following are the tools for periodicals selection:

1. Union list of serials
2. Ulrich's International Periodical Directory
3. Directory of Indian Scientific Periodicals
4. Reader's Guide to Periodical Literature
5. BLLD current serials

6. Guide to Indian Periodical Literature
7. Review of Journals
8. NIFOR guide to Indian Periodicals.

The librarian should follow the following collection development policy:

1. By purchase
2. By gift
3. By exchange.

Use and Maintenance of the Library

The basic objective of any library is to provide reading material to its users. Hence all the activities and functions of the library are based on the above objective only.

By taking into consideration the fundamental functions of a library, different sections are created. The following chart would explain each function with the section/s attached to it.

FUNCTIONS AND SECTIONS OF A LIBRARY

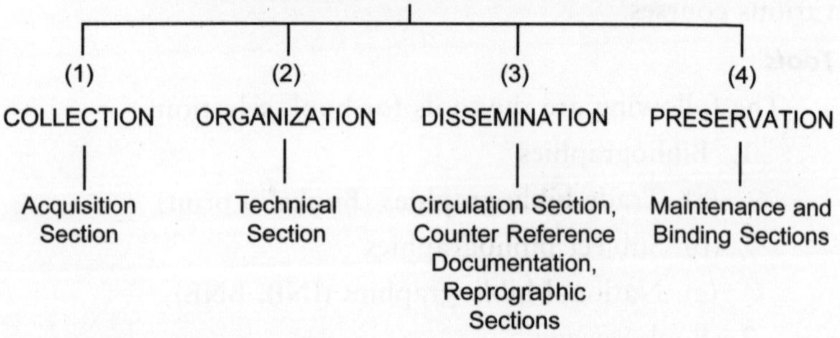

Acquisition Section

Dr. S.R. Ranganathan, while referring about the functions of a library, termed the work of acquisition and organization as 'behind the screen' and other functions as 'outside the screen'.

By 'behind the screen', he meant those jobs such as ordering, processing that are not done in the presence of the users and by 'outside the screen', he meant the jobs such as counter work, reference and other services that are done in direct contact with the readers.

The librarian, in the process of collection, purchases books directly within the reach of the funds allotted to the library. The purchase of books involves the following routines in the acquisition section:

1. Selection,
2. Ordering,
3. Accessioning, and
4. Bill passing.

The librarian, along with the selection committee, first selects the books by following the methods explained earlier. Then he formally sends the official order to acquire the books. After getting the books the librarian sends the books for accessioning —the accessioning involves writing of the serial number in the accession register along with the particulars such as date of purchase, name of the publisher, the supplier's details, page number, call number, price and the year of publication—then the librarian duly passes the bill for payment. The above works are undertaken in the acquisition section.

Technical Section

According to Dr. S.R. Ranganathan's fifth law of library science (a library is a growing organism), the main parts of the library that are capable of growing, are:

(i) the books,
(ii) the readers, and
(iii) the staff.

Innumerable books are being published daily all over the world and each library adds to its collection some books according to its selection procedure.

In the technical section, highly technical jobs such as classification and cataloguing are undertaken. According to Ranganathan, highly qualified persons should take charge of this section, since service to the users in providing right information at the right time depends upon the work done in this section. In other words, it is the classification which brings the auxiliary and related books placed next to the main books. For example, books on astronomy, differential equation and trigonometry would be arranged next to the main book, i.e. 'Mathematics', if only the classifier is efficient.

Accuracy and consistency should be strictly maintained in classification and cataloguing, otherwise the books on related subjects would be scattered and this would bring about confusion and the major objective of the library would be lost. It is the classifier who assigns call numbers to the books by making use of any standard scheme of classification system. After the call number (class number and book number) is assigned to a book it is sought by its call number. Before assigning the call number the classifier has to check the catalogue cards, whether the book is a new one or a duplicate one. If the book is a second copy, the classifier has to mention it in the call number in the following manner:

Title	Call No.
1. Basic Education John (A)....1982	TN3 M2 (First Copy)
2. Basic Education John (A)....1982	TN3 M2-1 (Second Copy)

This has been dealt with in detail in the chapter on 'Classification'.

After the classification, the books would be sent for cataloguing. The cataloguer, by following either CCC or AACR should decide the number of entries according to the type of the book and the policy of the library. The cataloguer must have a sound knowledge in principles of cataloguing. Before making any attempt, the cataloguer has to check in the library whether any such type of book is available or not. If the book is already available in the library, the new book with different edition should be consolidated with the author and title cards already available with the library. Only a main card has to be prepared for the new edition or for a duplicate book. If necessary, the cataloguer has to provide cross reference and analytical entries. After the classification and the cataloguing, the books are sent for pasting which includes pasting of data tables, round slips for call number and book pocket to hold book's card.

Circulation Section

Normally services in a library may be broadly divided into two. They are:

(a) Reader services and

(b) Auxiliary services.

The reader's services include circulation, inter-library loan and reference service for study and research in the library. And the auxiliary services include documentation, such as translation, photocopying, indexing, abstracting, audio-visual aids and extension activities.

Circulation refers to the activity of a library in lending books to borrowers and keeping records of the loans. In other words, that part of library service which is concerned with the circulation of books and other reading material is known as circulation section or the lending section. This is the most popular section of the library.

The term 'circulation' also refers to the total number of volumes, including pamphlets and periodicals, loaned during a given period of time for use outside the library. According to Americans the term circulation work indicates, the work of the department issuing books for home-reading.

The following works are being undertaken in the circulation section:

(i) Registration of members.

(ii) Issuing and returning of books (charging and discharging).

(iii) Charging overdues (overdues fine).

(iv) Reservation of books; inter-library loan.

(v) Sending reminders.

(vi) Renewal of books (extension).

(vii) Issuing duplicate tickets.

(viii) Withdrawal of membership.

(ix) Records maintenance work which includes preparing statistics and other miscellaneous work.

Charging and Discharging

The circulation of books takes place at the counter, where books move in and out of the library, hence the counter is the heart of the library. Majority of the users love taking books home. Different categories of users are entitled to get varying number of books for a given period of time. These books can be re-issued for another loan period on presentation of the books at the counter, if they are not in demand. It is known as 'extension of books'.

The term 'charging' is the record of loan, giving particulars of the book lent and the reader's name and address. In other words charging is 'to issue a book' and 'to record the loan of the book'.

In olden days the libraries were considered as storehouses and only a few privileged people were issued books. Thanks to the invention of printing press and the resulting increase in publication of books resulted in the reduction in prices of the books. This enabled the libraries to issue books to the users.

Initially, the books were issued by mentioning the bibliographical details of the book and the details of the reader to whom the book had been issued in a ledger. The number of libraries, books and readers increased in due course. As a result, the older charging systems like Day Book system and Ledger system were replaced by Card system.

There are different types of charging systems in use. They are:

(a) Day book system
(b) Ledger system
(c) Machine charging system
(d) Dummy system
(e) Temporary system
(f) Card system
(g) Browne charging system
(h) Newark charging system
(i) Ranganathan's Reader's Ticket, Book Ticket Methods
(j) Computerised circulation control system.

(a) **Day book system.** Initially books were issued by entering the bibliographical details of the book and the reader's particulars in a notebook. It was found useful since the users were limited in number.

(b) **Ledger system.** In this system a register is maintained and each reader is allotted one or two pages. It contains the reader's name and address and some columns that are to be filled at the time of issue and return of books. The accession number, call number, author, title, due date and the signature of the borrower are generally filled in the register.

Though this system provides a permanent record of the borrower and the books, it is difficult to search for a particular book which has been issued to any reader.

(c) **Machine charging system.** The developed countries use the following mechanised charging and discharging methods:

1. Photocharging method.
2. Audiocharging method.

In the first category charging is done by placing the membership card and the book to be borrowed in the microfilm. When the machine is on, the book and the borrower's particulars are filmed. Then the book along with the borrower's card is given to the reader. It is rather a costly affair and the charging work disrupts when the machine fails.

The audiocharging is similar to photocharging method. Here the information or the borrower and the book to be borrowed are dictated into a dictation machine and this information is recorded on tapes of recording discs. Since the information is stored in tapes the location of a particular book is difficult, since it requires the whole tape to be played to locate the same.

(d) **Dummy system.** To solve the problems posed by the ledger system, the Dummy system was introduced. As the name suggests, each book on the shelves is provided a wooden dummy of the average size of the book. When the book is issued, the dummy occupies the place of the book on the shelf. It is a cumbersome method of charging.

(e) **Temporary slip system.** The Temporary slip system was introduced as a result of disadvantages of the Dummy system. In this system, slips are used to borrow books. The reader has to fill his name and address along with the bibliographical details of the book in the slip. The due date is stamped on the slip and the book is issued. The slips are arranged either by the name of the borrower or by the call number of the book. Though this system is quite easy and has less problems, yet it could not work for long.

(f) **Card system.** As the temporary slip system was working well, cards were introduced in place of slips, which could withstand wear and tear. Here only one card was used, as a result, the library personnel had to note down the details of the borrower and the book only. This resulted in the introduction of two card system in libraries—one card for the book and one for the reader. This resulted in the introduction of the two most important charging systems known as (1) Browne and (2) Newark which are discussed in greater detail.

(g) **Computerised circulation control system.** The computerised charging and discharging system was first introduced by the American Library Association in 1947. Here each borrower is given a code number and a book is issued or returned by making use of the accession number of the book already entered in the computer. With the recent advance in science and technology, the code number is converted into a bar code and the book is charged or discharged with the help of bar code reader. The advantages of the computer control system are its speed and accuracy.

The following are the important charging systems currently in use:

1. Newark charging system
2. Browne charging system
3. Ranganathan's Reader's Ticket, Book Ticket Methods.

Newark Charging System

This method of recording book loans is widely used in America. It was introduced in the United States in 1900. In this system, each user is issued a borrower's card mentioning the details of registration number, name, address, etc. To get a book issued, the user has to present the book along with the borrower's card. The circulation assistant withdraws the book card from the book pocket and notes down the registration number on it and puts the stamp of the due date on the book card, date slip and the borrower's card. The borrower's card along with the book is returned to the user.

To return the book, the user presents the book and the borrower's card at the discharging counter. The counter assistant will search for the relevant book card from the charging tray and replace it in the book pocket. The date of return would be stamped on the book card, date slip and the borrower's card.

Browne Charging System

The 'Browne charging system' was started by Nina E. Browne. It is a single-entry method of recording book loans. It uses a pocket bearing the borrower's name to hold the book card. This system is little used in Western countries but it is very popular in Indian libraries.

In this system each reader is given borrower's cards bearing pockets to hold the book cards of the books issued out. The cards bear the details of the user, registration number, name and address of the user. The book card bears the call number, author and title.

When a user desires to get a book issued, he presents the book along with the borrower's card. The counter assistant removes the book card from the book and inserts it in the borrower's card. Then he stamps the due date on the date slip, and returns the book only. He retains the borrower's card to be arranged in the charging tray.

While returning the book, the reader presents the book at the discharging window. The counter assistant would trace out the book card from the tray and withdraw the book card from the borrower's card and replace it in the book pocket and return the borrower's ticket to the reader.

Ranganathan's Charging System

'Ranganathan's charging system' is just the reverse of Browne System. In this system, the book card is removed from the book pocket and the borrower's ticket is slipped in the book card. After stamping the due date on the date slip, the book is returned to the reader.

While returning the book, the counter assistant traces out the book card arranged in the due date tray and removes the borrower's card from the book card. The book card is replaced in the book pocket and the borrower's card is returned to the reader.

The main difference between Ranganathan's and Browne's system is that in the former system the book card holds the borrower's card, whereas in the latter the borrower's card holds the book card.

Maintenance Section

The maintenance section is equally important in enabling the librarian to run the library, smoothly. It is in this section that all mending works are undertaken. The work of this section is related to almost all the sections of the library. The following works are done in this section:

1. Cards, filing
2. Shelving work
3. Stock verification
4. Preservation of reading material
5. Binding work
6. Weeding out unserviceable books
7. Other minor works like repair of building equipments and so on.

Filing and Shelving

From the technical section, the books are sent to the maintenance section, where the catalogue cards are first arranged and filed in the relevant trays. The book is then sent to the relevant section to be arranged on the shelf properly. These works should be done systematically without any delay, otherwise, the readers would not get the books they require.

Stock Verification

Stock verification refers to the process of taking stock by checking records of books possessed along with the number of copies on the shelves or on loan. It involves a physical verification or check of each book in stock according to the accession register.

Several practising librarians throughout the world differ radically on the issue of 'stock verification'. It is generally felt that in view of the ever growing large holdings in libraries, the task of stock-taking is sheer waste of time of library staff while some others insist on 'sample stock-taking'.

Aim

The primary aim of stock-taking is to ascertain if all the books that have been stocked in the library can be accounted for. Hence the service libraries carry out stock verification of their books once a year.

Purpose

The stock verification helps the librarians in the following manner:

(i) It tells them how many books are actually lost during a certain period.

(ii) It helps in stock rectification by restoring the misplaced books at their proper places.

(iii) It helps the authority to know if the library staff is careless, negligent or even dishonest.

(iv) It helps the authority to see physically the conditions of the books, and the damaged books can then be sent for repair.

(v) It helps in replacing the lost books.

Stock verification can be done by adopting any one of the following methods:

1. By accession register
2. By numerical counting

3. By shelf register/list cards
4. By accession number sheets.

Stock verification by accession register is a cumbersome job, since the books on the shelves are arranged according to the classified order and each time the pages of the register have to be turned to suit the accession number of the book.

The numerical counting is the simplest method of stock verification since it involves the counting of the books on the stacks plus the books lent on loan and this number is compared with the total number in the accession register. The balance indicates the loss of books. But this system will not help us in pointing out the particular books which have been lost and does not serve the basic purpose of stock verification.

The stock verification by shelf register/list cards is the best method, since these cards are prepared and maintained only for this purpose. These cards are arranged in a tray according to the classified order. When the call number of the book is read out the corresponding card would be removed and kept in a separate tray. The remaining cards would tell us the exact books missing.

In India, normally, the librarian has to take the responsibility of loss of books, and he has to pay for it. It was Dr. S.R. Ranganathan who suggested that in an open access library, an annual loss of three volumes for every 1000 books issued should be written off. The UGC library-committee recommended to write off 2 books for every 1000 books issued. But in developed countries such practices are not followed and they simply write off the books lost in the stock verification.

Preservation of Reading Material

The term preservation is the maintenance of objects close to their original condition as far as possible, or until they are no longer needed. According to Rufus Choate, "the book is the only immortality", hence it is the duty of the librarian to see that rare books and archive material get preserved from the environmental, physical, chemical and biological factors.

One of the functions of preservation is to collect the documents of the past and the present and to keep and maintain them so that they are available to both present and future users.

Before making any attempt to preserve the information materials, they must be first protected from their enemies such as insects which include termites, cockroaches, silverfish, book worms, mud wasp, rats and mice. These insects can be controlled by making use of the following insect control system:

1. Anti-termite control—D.D.T., Gammexane.
2. Fumigation—Hydrocyanic gas and methyl bromide.

In the first, antitermite chemicals like D.D.T. and Gammexane may be sprayed to control insects.

In the second, by fumigation of gases, the insects may be controlled considerably, it is unanimously agreed that fumigation is the best insect controlling system. Normally in a big library, a small room which can be made air tight, is converted into a fumigation chamber. The books are placed on wooden planks, then chemicals like carbo-oxide and methyl bromide are placed in a corner. These chemicals start evaporating and producing light fumes. The books should be allowed to remain in the fumigation chamber for at least three days.

The modern method of preservation is to convert the reading materials which are worn out, into micro form, microfiche and microopaque. The other ways of preserving valuable materials are to make xerox copies and the brittle papers may be laminated to save them from perishing.

Binding

Each library adds to its collection some reading materials according to its funds and policies. In turn, these books and periodicals are issued to readers for their use. In this process, wear and tear of the reading material is inevitable. Some material not of lasting value is weeded out or discarded but at the same time, there are some books which are repaired for the constant use of readers.

The term 'repair' here means the binding of books and periodicals. A big library normally has its own binding section. But a considerable number of libraries get their materials bound through the commercial book binders. Binding is also a process of preserving books. As the proverb goes, 'a stitch in time saves nine', unless any worn out or damaged book is bound in time, it is not possible to preserve it. The following are the reasons that necessitate binding:

1. To preserve perishable and frail materials.
2. To resist wear and tear.
3. To avoid damage from rough handling.
4. To give a new look.

The librarian, after deciding the books to be sent for binding, has to give instructions to the binder regarding the type of binding applicable to his library. The following are the types of bindings:

1. Paperback binding.
2. Reinforced binding.
3. Half-leather binding.
4. Full-leather binding.
5. Full-cloth binding.
6. Half-cloth binding.
7. Edition binding.

Books are our great friends. We must treat them with full regards and should save them from injuries and injurious elements.

Weeding Out

We are living in an age of 'information explosion'; thousands of books and periodicals are being published everyday throughout the world. They are being used constantly by millions of readers, as a result, the books get worn out, and become obsolete and out of date. This results in withdrawing the unserviceable reading material from the circulation in the library. This is known as weeding out or discarding of books.

In other words, weeding out is the practice of discarding or transferring to storage superfluous copies, rarely used books and material no longer of use.

A UGC report on 'weeding out' says, "Many works lose their value within one generation, say in twenty-five years. By that time, their thought content becomes outmoded. The thought content of some may even turn out to be wrong. In a service library, no useful purpose is served by retaining such pedestrian books and providing shelf space to them after they have become obsolete. The proper course is to weed them out periodically. They should give place to their current variations."

Normally the year books, annuals and books of older editions are published every year with up-to-date information. As new editions replace the older editions, they have to be weeded out or discarded periodically. In addition to this, books and periodicals mutilated by readers should be written off.

Library Committee

A library committee is defined as, "the committee responsible for the management of a library". In other words, it refers to the committee which is responsible for provision of library services.

The library committee consists of a group of persons who are empowered to do certain jobs relating to library administration. The library committee includes a chairman, members and a convenor or a secretary. The general policies of administration of a library are laid down by the committee, while the librarian is responsible for seeing that the policies are carried out. The librarian should always be its ex-officio secretary.

Need for the Library Committee

The following are the needs for the establishment of library committee:

1. The committee as a representative body can achieve things easily for the development of the library.
2. It helps the librarian in the smooth functioning of the library.
3. The committee can help the librarian to achieve his objectives politically.

Functions of Library Committee

1. To formulate and plan policies of the library in relation to the development of resources for instruction and research.
2. To advise regarding the allocation of book funds to the library.

3. To develop a general programme of library service for all in the interests of the institution.
4. To review the progress, annual reports, accounts and annual budgets.

Library Personnel Management

For the success of any institution, the persons who work for it are the most important. The term personnel administration is defined as, "that activity which directs human resources into a kind of dynamic organization which accomplishes its goals through provision of opportunities for maximum individual contribution under desirable working relationships and conditions; it includes selection, allocation, utilization and development of employees, as well as improvement of working conditions to obtain maximum productivity and efficiency under specially emphasized consideration for individual and human demands".

In other words, personnel management is the use of human resources in accomplishing the overall goals or mission of the organization.

It is a general fact that libraries in India are facing the general problems of budget and shortage of staff. Hence, a librarian must have sound knowledge of the principles of efficient personnel management. The personnel manager should try to develop *esprit de corps* among the workers. The team spirit is very essential in libraries where one work is dependent on the other.

The following are the steps involved in the process of personnel management:

1. Human resource planning and forecasting.
2. Recruitment.
3. Selection.
4. Training and development.
5. Performance appraisal.
6. Promotion and demotion.

Library Finance and Budget

It is a general fact that library is not a revenue fetching department. It is a spending institution. It depends on the funds allotted by the government as well as its parent body. Its financial demands are recurring and keep increasing every year, since a library is a growing organism.

Hence proper financial resources should be made available to meet the recurring and growing needs of the library. This implies that the librarian should judicially allocate funds and prepare budget to provide a balanced collection to the users. Though libraries in India face financial problems, it is the duty of the librarian to maximise the minimum funds allotted.

Sources of Library Finance

A library has a few sources of income to meet the ever growing expenditure and to balance its budget. The sources of income are:

1. Grants
2. Gifts and endowments
3. Subscription fees
4. Fines and service charges
5. Rents and sales.

The major portion of the library's financial requirements are met by grants from the Government. The Government provides funds to the library through tax collected in the form of library cess. For university and college libraries, the UGC allocates considerable amount in the form of matching grants.

Another source of income is from endowments, though only a few libraries receive such funds. Occasionally some individual philanthropist foundations give funds to libraries. For instance, the Delhi University Library receives book grants from the Ford Foundation. And under PL 480 programme, several university libraries in India received funds for the purchase of reading materials.

The library also gets funds in the form of subscription fees, fines and service charges. In addition, the library gets some funds by selling the publications and by renting the library hall for cultural functions.

Budget

To have an effective maintenance of library finance, it is essential to prepare an annual budget. The budget is the total amount of money which is available for library purposes after the estimate of anticipated needs has been approved by the appropriate authority.

The budget is a comprehensive document, containing the detailed estimates of and the plans for the financial transactions which are needed by the organization to carry out its programme effectively during a fiscal period.

According to Louis Round Wilson and Maurice F. Tauber, a budget is, "a financial statement of the estimated revenues and expenditure of an institution for a definite period of time". In general, it is an estimate of the revenue and expenditure for future and it is a plan to balance the income and expenditure. It can be used as an effective control device.

Functions of a Budget

1. The budget is considered as an effective tool to limit the expenditure and to see that it does not exceed the limit.
2. It helps to identify proper priorities in spending, so as to achieve maximum utility of the money.
3. It coordinates entire activities of the library.
4. It helps the librarian to learn from past experiences and the librarian can analyse the mistakes and take steps to avoid them in future.
5. The library budget is based on the following formula Capital – Expenditure = Effective Programmes or Service.

Preparation of a Budget

The library-budget is prepared by or under the direction of the librarian. He has to present and defend it before his Board or Library Committee, or any other authority, whom the institution nominates.

There are three ways in which the librarian can prepare the budgetary estimates. They are:

1. By comparison with past expenditure.
2. By budgeting in accordance with the work programme.
3. By using arbitrary standards and rules.

'Arbitrary standards' means to set the ratio of library expenditure to the total budget of an institution. It also means to work cut the exact amount to be spent per student, per faculty member, on books, journals, staff and maintenance of other public services in a library.

The Budget Allocation

The Kothari Education Commission Report (1964-66) had suggested around 6.5 per cent of educational budget as reasonable expenditure on libraries. It also suggested that as a norm, a university should spend each year about Rs. 25 per student and Rs. 300 per teacher.

The main budget heads are:

1. The staff salaries
2. Books and journals and
3. Miscellaneous expenditures (stationery, cards, communication, postages, etc.)

With regard to the distribution of expenditure, B.M. Headicar has worked out the items and the percentage of funds to be spent:

1. Books	17.0%
2. Binding	6.7%
3. Journals	4.0%
4. Salaries	44.0%
5. Rent/loans	8.2%
6. Other expenditure	20.1%
	100.0%

Three types of budgets commonly used in libraries are:

1. Line budget (traditional budget).

2. Programme planning and budgeting system.
   (It is commonly used in non-profit organizations.)
3. Zero base budget (involves a cost benefit analysis).

(a) *The Line Budget*. The line budget is a traditional and commonly used one. It consists of two basic categories, namely, the capital expenses and the recurring expenses. Normally, the library budget covering the recurring expesnes is prepared annually.

The capital expenses include the amount spent on equipments like typewriters, furniture, etc. and the construction of a new library building.

The following are the drawbacks of the line budget:

(i) The funds once allotted, are fixed and the expenses should not exceed the fixed amount.

(ii) The amount allotted has to be spent by the month of March. This would hamper in the selection of good books.

(b) *Programme Planning and Budgeting System* (*PPBS*). The Programme Planning and Budgeting System was introduced by Charles Hitch in 1961 in the Department of Defence of the U.S. As it was a success it was used in education, health and library management. While the line budget allocates funds on the basis of fixed heads, in PPBS it is according to programmes introduced to attain goals set in the plan. It is a method of budgeting based on a system approach that enables managers to think and plan well into the future, analyse costs and benefits of the existing programmes and find better and cheaper ways to achieve the objectives.

(c) *Zero Base Budget* (*ZBB*). Zero base budgeting was introduced in Texas Instruments Inc., in 1970 by Peter Pyhrr. It was introduced as a means to achieve more effective fiscal control in non-profit organizations. It involves allocation of funds to organizations on the basis of cost-benefit analysis of each activity of the organization. The advantages of the Zero base budget are:

1. If offers alternatives in the selection of packages.

2. Only those activities that can be justified are included in the budget.
3. The relationship between the quality and level of service to be provided and the cost of providing it is well established.

Very few libraries in India make use of this type of budget.

Library Statistics and Annual Reports

Library Statistics

The evaluation of libraries on the basis of opinions expressed by the users has been an effective one. But with the emergence of statistical methods, the library and information science started using the quantitative measures to evaluate the performance of libraries.

Maintenance of statistics in a library is most essential. It is generally accepted that it is on the basis of these statistics that the progress of a library is evaluated and judged. The statistics can assist in streamlining the entire administration of a library.

One of the most important advantages of maintaining statistics is that they are of immense value for the preparation of the annual report.

To sum up, the librarian requires statistics for the following purposes:

1. To compile annual report.
2. To measure efficiency of different sections.
3. To plan for the efficient services.

On the basis of the statistics, a new service can be planned or an existing service can be improved. These statistics enable the authority in getting a clear picture about the functioning of a library. This, in turn, helps the librarian in getting funds and staff to improve the existing services.

The library statistics can be broadly classified into two categories:

1. Statistical and
2. Organizational.

The statistical data include the work done daily or weekly by the library personnel working in various technical sections of the library. The organizational statistics include:

(a) budget,

(b) personnel,

(c) visitors, and

(d) cultural activities.

Annual Report

Any organization is expected to present its annual report. The annual report is the survey of work carried out during the preceding year. It is the administrative report of the library to be presented to the higher authorities. The annual report summarizes the activities and achievements of the library of the previous year.

Need

The librarian is expected to present the annual report to his higher authorities/library committee to keep them informed periodically, of the achievements and activities of the library. It is an effective tool for the librarian in seeking support from the higher authorities in terms of men and money.

The annual report also serves as a publicity material. The activities and services rendered by the library would attract and encourage readers to visit the library frequently. It is an effective yardstick to measure the improvement of the library. This report enables the librarian in setting right the shortcomings that might have prevailed in the library.

Compilation

The annual report should be presented in a simple and lucid manner, so that even a layman is able to understand the matter. The statements should be short and clear, and slang and jargon must be avoided. The period of the report may be either the calendar year or the financial year which depends upon the custom of the parent body.

Classification

6

The term 'Library Classification' is a process of putting books and other reading materials on a subject in a logical sequence on the shelves which could be helpful to the readers. Classification is one of the most important steps in the organization of libraries and has been rightly called the foundation of librarianship. Sayers has rightly remarked that, "The foundation of the library is the book and the foundation of librarianship is classification."

According to Sayers, classification is, "the arrangement of books on shelves, or description of them in a manner which is most useful to those who read". Classification is probably the foundation on which is based the superstructure of library science. In fact, it is classification which gives library science the character of a 'science'.

Historically speaking, the Indian and the ancient Greek philosophers had worked out schemes for classification of knowledge. Some good schemes for library classification were developed during the late 19th century and 20th century, viz.:

1. Dewey decimal classification (1876)
2. Expansive classification (1891-93)
3. Subject classification (1906)
4. Library of Congress classification (1904)
5. Bibliographic classification (1935)
6. Colon classification (1933)
7. Universal decimal classification (1905).

Need and Purpose of Library Classification

The main purpose of library classification is to "place books in relation to one another from the viewpoint of the reader". It is generally accepted that every book deals with one or more areas of knowledge. But in library classification we have to find out the most dominant subject, for, books are to be arranged in a linear order on shelves according to that dominant subject. The arrangement should bring books, which have a likeness, together on the shelves.

A library contains recorded knowledge in the form of books and non-book materials. The problem is how they can be arranged. The arrangement may be made by size, author, title, etc. It is true that unless the relation between the library materials is known and clearly established, full use of the resources of a library cannot be made. Hence, it is the primary task of a librarian to ensure the maximum utilisation of the collection and to see that the resources of the library are arranged and displayed in a helpful manner.

Different factors are considered for determining the arrangement of material in a library. Of these, the most significant feature is the principle of arrangement by the thought content of the material. If books are arranged primarily on the basis of author or the title, we get books on the subject of our interest, whose authors or title we know, but miss other books on the same subject. Hence, the classification is done by the thought content of the material.

Essentials of Library Classification

The library classification is a process of translating the specific subject of a book into an artificial language of ordinal numbers, which, in classificatory language, are helpful in arriving at a logical arrangement.

The essential components of a scheme of library classification are:

(a) notations,

(b) form divisions,

(c) form classes,

(d) generalia class, and

(e) index.

Notation

The 'notations' are the symbols which stand for the divisions in a scheme of classification. In other words, notation is a set of symbols which stand for a class or subject (e.g. philosophy, literature) and its subdivisions (e.g. Ethics, English literature) representing a scheme of classification. For the purpose of arranging books, use of names of the subjects, broad or specific, in natural language would neither be practical nor convenient; so these are translated into artificial language of ordinal numbers.

Hence, the term notation has been defined as, 'any set of symbols or characters to denote things or relations in order to facilitate the recording of them'. It is the ordered series of symbols that stand for the ordered series of terms in the classification schedules.

Four sets of symbols are used:

(i) For main class names,

(ii) For isolate terms,

(iii) For literary form divisions, and

(iv) For connecting symbols (phase relation, etc.).

In appearance there are two types of notation. They are:

1. Pure
2. Mixed.

A pure notation consists of only one type of symbol, e.g., either numerals like 1, 2, 3, 4, 5, 6, 7, 8, 9, etc., or letters a, b, c, d, e,...z or A, B, C, D, E,...Z. In mixed notation, more than one set of symbols are used (numerical, alphabetical, etc.).

The pure notation is easy to understand, but the mixed notation is easier to remember and increases the capacity of the scheme of library classification. Most notations are of the mixed variety. Bliss and Richardson recommended mixed notation. Dr. S.R. Ranganathan uses mixed notation in his Colon classification. But Melvil Dewey in his Dewey decimal classification uses pure notation of numbers, which is relatively simple and can easily convey order/arrangement to us.

Mathematically, a notation may be said to be of two types, namely, integral and decimal. The integral notation consists of integers. The decimal notation is conceived decimally, in other words, no figure is read as an integer, but as a decimal fraction. Therefore, 11, 12 should be considered as 1.1, 1.2. Numerals are used decimally so as to permit the logical subdivision of subjects or a chain of classes indefinitely.

Functions of Notation

1. The main aim of notation is to consolidate the preferred order of a classification scheme. It should help to maintain the sequence of subjects mechanically by giving each term a symbol possessing an agreed ordinal value.

2. It serves to connect the alphabetical order of index with the systematic order of schedule. By consulting the number attached to the index entry, one can locate the subject in the classification schedule. Notation thus makes the alphabetical subject index effective.

3. It allows mechanical reference to be made from any catalogue entry to the material on the shelves.

4. It serves as a key to the organization and structure of the classification schedule.

Form Divisions

Form divisions are the 'adjuncts to a classification which enable books to be arranged within their subject according to the form in which they are written. They usually have mnemonic notation which can be applied to any part of a scheme.' Knowledge may be presented in books in one form or the other. The form could be textbook, manual, history, dictionary, encyclopaedia, etc. The book classification takes care of representing form in the call numbers.

The numbers representing forms of book are generally called form divisions and since they are commonly shared by all subjects they are also known as common subdivisions or common isolates. In other words, form divisions are divisions of any main class or any subject. A book on a particular subject may deal with that subject from various standpoints and outer and inner forms, e.g. from the standpoint inner form of history or philosophy or in the outer form of a dictionary, encyclopaedia, periodical, essay or other literary form.

Form Classes

Form classes 'are those parts of a classification in which the books are arranged according to the form in which they are written such as poetry, drama, fiction, essays, etc.'

The 'form class' accommodates books in which the main interest is the form of presentation or the literary pattern in which matter is written, as in poetry, drama, letters, etc. The form class proper is the Belle letters class or Literature class. In this class, form is the primary interest and the subject matter of the books is ignored.

The arrangement of the divisions of the form class differs in different classification schemes. Dewey arranges literature into language in which the books are written, then into forms of presentation—poetry, drama, etc., and finally into chronological order.

Generalia Class

There are certain books such as *Encyclopaedia Britannica*, *Bibliography* or collected writings of Mahatma Gandhi, which cannot be classed under any specific subject for they could and do cover all subjects under the sun. The classification schemes provide generalia class, for such books. In other words, the generalia class is called the main class of a classification. This is reserved for general books and it accommodates materials on all or many branches of knowledge, whose subject content is not restricted to any one subject. For example, in Colon classification, Dr. S.R. Ranganathan includes in the generalia class subjects like Exposition, Library Science, Gazetteers, etc.

Index

'An index is an alphabetical list of the terms mentioned in the schedule, with the corresponding notations attached.' It includes all the synonyms of these terms, together with the minute parts of a subject even if they are not included in the schedule.

In other words, an 'alphabetical index' in a classification scheme locates terms in the classification and it may also bring together related aspects of a subject which may have been scattered by the classified sequence. According to Sayers, "The index is the alphabetical key to the systematic order of the classification scheme."

The 'index' is necessary because in a classification scheme the terms or class-names are not in the alphabetical order but in a preferred order. The index guides a reader from the natural name of the subject to the artificial name and thus helps him to find the appropriate place occupied by the subject in the classification scheme. It also helps a classifier to assign class-numbers to books.

Hence the index is an essential component of a scheme of library classification. It is provided at the end of the scheme. It is of great use to the members in their handling of the classified part of a catalogue. There are two kinds of index, namely, 'The Relative Index' (DDC) and 'The Specific Index' (subject classification).

Call Number

According to, 'Terminology of Documentation' of UNESCO, the call number is, 'a number used to indicate the location of a book on the shelves'. In other words, it is a set of letters, numerals, and/or other symbols providing complete identification of an individual work and its relative location. It consists of class and book number and sometimes of such other data as date, volume number, copy number, location symbol, etc.

Usually the call number is followed by the book number or simply the author mark. It is used to identify a particular book, and to indicate both its position on the shelves and its position relative to other books. It is marked on the lower part of the spine of a book as well as on catalogue cards and other records.

In the Colon classification, the call number consists of the class number, book number and collection number. The call number fixes the position of a book's specific subject relative to other subjects. It mechanizes the position or seat of a volume/document on the shelf. With the help of the call number, a book is quickly taken out of and restored to its position. For example, the call number for the title 'The Indian Education'—1975, would be 370.954 L5 in DDC.

370.954	–	class number for Indian Education.
L5	–	book number (published in 1975).

Book Number

The classification of library material does not end with the assignment of the notation for the subject of a book or document, i.e. the assignment of class-number.

When several books have exactly the same class number, it is necessary to fix the position of each individual book or volume for mechanically placing it on the shelf. This process is called individualization of books, and the symbols used for individualization are collectively termed 'book number'.

A book number represents author or year of publication. Some classification schemes such as CC, SC, BC recommend that books under the same specific class be arranged according to the year of publication, it is also known as 'chronological mark'.

Schemes of Library Classification

At the close of the 19th century librarians began to think seriously about the problem of arrangement of their book-stocks and they related classification more to physical books than to the thought content or subject of books. With the advent of the ideas of Melvil Dewey and Charles Ammi Cutter, the library field took a new turn since they gave importance to classification by thought content rather than physical.

The classification schemes mostly used in India are:

1. Dewey decimal classification,
2. Universal decimal classification, and
3. Colon classification.

Dewey Decimal Classification

Dewey decimal classification is probably the most popular of all modern library classification schemes. It was devised by Melvil Dewey (1851-1931) in 1876 at the age of twenty-five. The first edition of the DDC was a slim volume of 42 pages, consisting of 12 pages of introductory matter, 12 pages of tables and 18 pages of index. The tables enumerated 1000 subjects and the index contained 2600 entries.

The subsequent editions have been the product of constant revision and expansion. The 14th edition, published in 1912, was the 'fullest' one. The 15th edition (1951) was a drastic revision and virtually an abridged edition. The 20th edition, with the addition of latest subjects, is now available in the market.

The DDC is enumerative in character and it is based on the principle of hierarchy, on the relationship between the general and the specific. It provides systematic arrangement in libraries of all materials mechanised by notation of great simplicity and apparent flexibility.

The surveys made by the ALA show that more than 96 per cent of public libraries and 89 per cent of college libraries in the U.S. use this system of classification. It is also used in most of the libraries in India and Europe. Besides, because of its simplicity, it is popular amongst readers also. The DDC is probably the most popular scheme of book classification. Its author divides the field of human knowledge into nine large classes, which he calls the First Summary Classes. In the Second and the Third Summary are the divisions and sections, respectively.

The whole universe of knowledge is taken as unity and divided into the following ten classes:

000	General works
100	Philosophy
200	Religion
300	Social Sciences
400	Language
500	Pure Sciences

600	Technology
700	The Arts
800	Literature
900	History & Geography

Each of the above ten classes is further divided into ten main divisions, e.g. 300 Social Sciences has the following divisions:

300	Social Sciences
310	Statistics
320	Political Science
330	Economics
340	Law
350	Public Administration
360	Social Problems and Services
370	Education
380	Commerce (trade)
390	Customs, etiquette, folklore.

Each of these divisions are further subdivided and so on, e.g.:

330	Economics
331	Labour Economics
332	Financial Economics
333	Land Economics
334	Cooperatives
335	Socialism and related systems
336	Public Finance
337	International Economics
338	Production
339	Macroeconomics and related topics.

As a matter of fact, all are decimal fraction notation, but for convenience of remembering the number, the decimal point is inserted after the third digit. Subdivisions are carried out decimally, and all numbers are read as decimals. At each stage there are nine coordinate divisions. Whenever there are more than nine divisions of equal status, the first eight are named and the remaining are covered in the ninth division 'Others'.

Universal Decimal Classification (UDC)

During first 'International Conference on Bibliography' held at Brussels in 1895, it was decided to have a scheme of classification for use in indexing world literature. The existing schemes of classification were found inadequate for the purpose, however, DDC was found flexible enough to be expanded and accepted as a base. Thus UDC is an international extension and adaptation of DDC initially done by two Belgians—Paul Otlet and Henri La Fontaine. The first edition appeared in French in 1905. Full edition in English was begun in 1943, and was titled 'Universal Decimal Classification'. The abridged editions were published in 1961 in 13 different languages.

Principles

The UDC was mainly developed for the purpose of indexing or arranging enormous card bibliographies which included not only books but also all kinds of documents, periodicals, articles, patents, abstracts and micro documents.

The principles underlying the UDC are:

1. To follow the general pattern of the DDC schedules, i.e. the division of the whole human knowledge into ten main branches and so on,
2. To retain the use of the decimally conceived numerals, and
3. To introduce numerous synthetic devices—an auxiliary apparatus of connection and relation signs, lacking in the DDC, whereby all types of compound subjects can be represented through combination of symbols.

The UDC is universal in the sense:

1. It is a general scheme of classification, covering all fields of knowledge. It is not a patchwork of isolated self-sufficient specialised groupings but is an integrated pattern of correlated subjects.

2. It aims to specify any combination of concepts necessary whether derived from within a subject field, or between different subjects.
3. It is international because it removes all national and racial factors to separate common facts; the classification of subjects is unimpeded by any bias to the needs of one particular nation.

Schedules

The UDC consists of two categories of schedules:

(a) The main tables in which are set out the main classes 1 to 9 and the various series of special auxiliaries.

(b) The auxiliary tables in which are set out the common auxiliaries and connecting symbols.

One of the most important features of UDC is its list of auxiliary tables. It is an extension of the principle of synthesis. It also covers various aspects likely to appear as parts of several different subjects. They are as follows:

Symbol	Expressed as	Significance
+	plus	Connection of non-consecutive numbers
/	stroke	Connection of consecutive numbers
:	colon	Relation
[]	Square brackets	Relation (subordinate)
=	equals	Language
(0)	brackets nought	Form
(1-9)	brackets	Place
(=)	Brackets equals	Race and nationality
" "	inverted commas	Time
A-Z	A to Z	Individual subdivision
-	hyphen	Special analytical no.
.00	point double 0	Point of view
.0	point nought	Special analytical no.

The main purpose of deriving UDC from DDC was to make it a comprehensive scheme of classification suitable to classify all types of recorded information. This classification may be called a subject classification in the correct sense of the term. It is based on 'the principle of processing from the general to the more particular'. The notation used in the UDC consists of Arabic numerals.

Colon Classification

Colon classification was devised by Dr. S.R. Ranganathan. Its first edition appeared in 1933. Since then, it has been constantly revised and improved upon and its sixth edition appeared in 1963. The colon classification is one of the most systematic schemes of library classification, used in many libraries in India and in few libraries abroad as well.

The arrangement of colon classification is as follows:

1.	Preliminaries	
2.	Annexure	
3.	Part I	Rules
4.	Part II	Schedules of classification
5.	Part III	Schedules of classification and sacred books with special names.

In colon classification each part has got its own index. Besides, there are three separate indexes in Part II, viz., Geographical index, Botany; index to natural groups; and Zoology: index to natural groups.

The colon classification is an 'analytico synthetic classification'. Like the DDC and LC, the colon classification does not provide readymade class numbers for most subjects. Hence it is not an enumerative scheme.

Notation in CC

Notation or artificial language of the colon classification includes:

1. Roman alphabets both small (omitting i, o, l) and capitals
2. Arabic numerals

3. Symbols like (comma, inverted comma, colon and semi-colon) (),; <- ->
4. Greek letters

The colon classification makes use of mixed notation which includes Roman lower case and capital letters, Indian numerals and a series of punctuation marks and other symbols as conjunctions and indicators. All notations are decimal fractions with well defined ordinal values for each species so as to provide a filiatory sequence to documents on stacks.

Facet Analysis

The colon classification is a fully faceted classification. The reason behind it is that in this scheme each main class or basic subject has been analysed into its facets so that there is absolutely no need for enumerating any compound subject. According to Dr. S.R. Ranganathan, "A faceted scheme for classification consists of schedules of basic classes, common isolates and special isolates only." For example, a subject may have one or more aspects, e.g. the subject, 'Education' may have aspects such as 'elementary education', 'curriculum', etc. Here Education is the main class. The aspect of 'elementary education' is based on levels of education. The aspect 'curriculum' is based on problems of education.

The term 'facet' is a technical term, it means an 'aspect', 'dimension' or a 'characteristic'. A facet is the total of sub-classes obtained by dividing a subject into sub-classes on the basis of one aspect or characteristic. This facet analysis helps us to divide a subject into convenient and workable groups which share the same characteristics.

Fundamental Categories

The facet analyses of subjects led Ranganathan to devise the postulate of Five Fundamental Categories. These categories are the result of the discovery of relationships between the diverse characteristics that may form the bases of the division of any subject. In other words, any facet of a subject, that can be conceived of, is but an expression of one of the five fundamental categories.

A Fundamental category is a root concept to which a facet is related explicitly or implicitly. All characteristics which form the very basis of division of a subject can be grouped under these root concepts. Ranganathan postulates (assumes) that there are only five such fundamental categories, viz.:

1. Personality [P]
2. Matter [M]
3. Energy [E]
4. Space [S]
5. Time [T]

For brevity the categories are indicated by the initionym PMEST. In other words, Ranganathan has divided most of the subjects or main classes, according to these five fundamental categories.

The fifth category, 'Time' is the simplest among the five and it refers to anything happening in a particular unit of time, e.g. 1970, 1980, winter, autumn, etc.

The fourth category, 'Space' stands for a geographical area, e.g. Chennai, Tamil Nadu, India, U.S.A., etc.

The third category, 'Energy' refers to any action or process or operation or property or problem, e.g. the act of beating, sowing, teaching, curing, etc. Besides, it includes disease, function and structure.

The second category, 'Matter' occurs in those few subjects where the material used can form the basis of further subdivision. Ornament, for example, is made of 'material', e.g. gold, silver, wood, etc.

The first category, 'Personality' is obtained by 'residue method'. In other words, what remains after we have eliminated all the four categories of Time, Space, Energy and Matter, is the Personality of the subject.

It would be clear if you look into the example given below. It shows how different facets of a subject are the manifestation of these five fundamental categories.

'Production of aluminium coins in India in 1975.'

Main class	-	Economics
1975	-	Time (unit of period)
India	-	Space (geographical area)
Production	-	Energy (problem - action/operation)
Aluminium	-	Matter (material)
Coins	-	Personality (remaining facet)

In order to separate and identify these five fundamental categories, symbols/connecting signs are used. They are:

Sl.No.	Fundamental Category	Symbol used in Schedule	Connecting Symbols
1.	Personality	[P]	, Comma
2.	Matter	[M]	; Semi Colon
3.	Energy	[E]	: Colon
4.	Space	[S]	. Point
5.	Time	[T]	' Single inverted comma

It should be noted that every fundamental category is preceded by its respective connecting symbol/sign. However, in the case of 'Personality' facet [P], when it comes immediately after a main class or 'Energy' [E] facet, the connecting symbol (comma) is omitted.

Rounds and Levels

In any given subject the fundamental categories are liable to occur more than once. This has led Ranganathan to evolve the postulates of Rounds and Levels of manifestation. To illustrate this, the title 'Treatment of Disease' can be used. The terms, 'Treatment' and 'disease' are problems, hence they are the manifestation of the 'Energy' facet. Treatment follows disease, consequently their order is, Disease: Treatment. The colon classification terms first problem as First Round Energy or [E] and the second problem as Second Round Energy or [2E] facet.

The colon classification postulates that fundamental categories [P], [M], [E] may manifest themselves in more than one Round in a subject. Facets [P], [M] appearing before facet [E] are called first Round facets; and [P], [M] facets following facet [E] are known as [2P] and [2M], respectively, and so on.

Any of the fundamental categories except the facet [E] manifesting itself more than once in one and the same Round is termed as 'Level' and it is symbolically expressed in the following manner:

[P_2] or [1P_2] = Second Level of First Round Personality

[2M] = Second Level of Second Round Matter.

One of the unique contributions of Ranganathan to library classification is that his theory enables us to distinguish very clearly between knowledge and book classification. The knowledge classification deals with only one category of concepts or ideas at a time and is thus governed by the rules of logical division, while the book classification deals with more than one category at a time, since the subject of a document may, and often does consist of a basic subject plus several concepts from different categories.

Cataloguing

7

Library catalogue is a list of books and other reading materials available in a library.

The word 'Catalogue' has been derived from the Greek phrase 'Katalogos', 'Kata' meaning 'by' or 'according to' and 'logos' meaning 'order' or 'reasons'. Hence, catalogue is regarded as a "work in which contents are arranged in a reasonable way, in a particular order or according to a set of plan".

According to "Terminology of Documentation" of UNESCO, a catalogue is "an ordered compilation of bibliographic description and sufficient information to afford access to the documents".

It is an art of preparing an index to a library collection. It is a fundamental tool of the users to help them to make maximum use of the library. Classification determines the subject-wise location of the documents on the shelves, whereas catalogue enables the users to know what books are available in a library with the particulars of the author, title and location.

Purpose and Functions

The primary function of a library catalogue is to reveal the available resources to its readers and the staff by way of a record of books and non-book materials, such as micro-films, record players, manuscripts and maps in the library. It does so with the help of unit records prepared for each document under its subject, author, title, etc. It is generally felt that the majority of general users seek information by the author and the title.

By taking into consideration of all approaches of the users, the modern libraries gear themselves to meet them by providing multiple entries for each book under different headings such as subject entry, author entry, title entry, series entry, collaborated entry, etc. In the present electronic era, many changes have taken place in catalogue too, but the function of a library catalogue still remains unchanged from what was enunciated by C.A. Cutter, a hundred years ago.

The following are the objectives of a library catalogue as stated by C.A. Cutter:

1. To enable a person to find a book of which either:
   (a) the author
   (b) or the title
   (c) or the subject is known
2. To show what the library has:
   (a) by a given author
   (b) on a given subject
   (c) in a given kind of literature
3. To assist in choice of a book:
   (a) as to its edition (bibliographically)
   (b) as to its character (literary or topical).

Dr. S.R. Ranganathan in his book, "Five Laws of Library Science", enunciated the following objectives of a library catalogue:

(a) To promote the use of books
(b) To disclose to every reader his or her book
(c) To secure for every book its reader
(d) To save the time of the reader and for this purpose
(e) To save the time of the staff.

The basic function of a library catalogue is to ascertain accurately and rapid determination of whether or not an item known by the author or title is in the library and if so, where it may be found. It also helps to find out what materials the library possesses on a given subject, where they may be found and how they are related to one another.

According to Dr. S.R. Ranganathan, "Catalogue's sole function is to disclose to the reader all the holdings of the library on his topic of interest, from whatever angle he pursues it, in such an exact, intimate and expeditious way as satisfies all the laws of library science. The reader may want to know all the resources of the library on a particular topic or by a particular author or in a particular series or he may ask for a book of which he knows only the author or collaborator—editor, translator, commentator or illustrator or merely its series or the editor of its series, or the title or may even have some vague idea of its contents. The library catalogue is designed for this function. In this design each book is given many entries."

Physical Form of Catalogue

The following is the list of catalogue forms being used in libraries:

1. A conventional bound printed book type format
2. Printed 'pasted slip'
3. Sheaf—a loose leaf binder format
4. Visible index
5. Card format

Generally, the card form is used in all types of libraries all over the world, which contains or consists of unit entries on somewhat stiff cards of 12.5 × 7.5 cm standard size. The present catalogue card (see next page) is the gradual development of the fixed register used in the past.

1. First vertical line
2. Second vertical line
3. First horizontal line (nine horizontal lines in a standard card).

None of the aforesaid physical forms of catalogue can satisfy all considerations. Each form has got its strong and weak points. However, the card catalogue possesses the maximum flexibility, hence it is the most accepted one in use.

PHYSICAL FORM OF CARD CATALOGUE

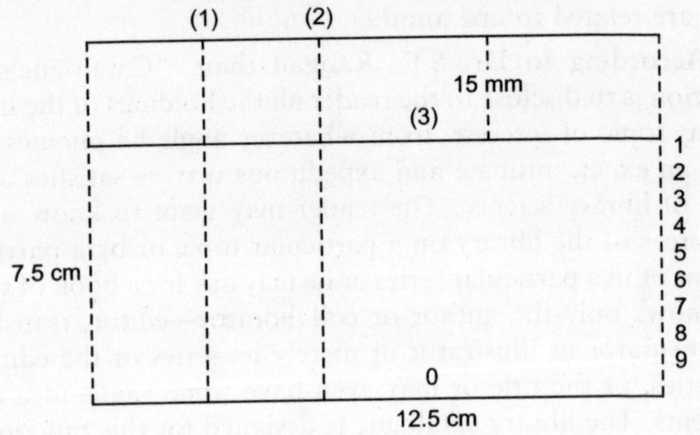

Types of Catalogue

There are three types of conventional catalogue on the basis of the inner or internal form of the catalogue. They are:

1. Dictionary Catalogue
2. Classified Catalogue
3. Divided Catalogue

Dictionary Catalogue

According to "Terminology of Documentation" of UNESCO, the dictionary catalogue is, "a catalogue of entries under authors, editors, translators, etc., titles, subjects and series which together with the necessary references are arranged in general alphabetical sequence".

In a dictionary catalogue all the entries (author, titles, subjects, series, etc.) and reference get arranged in a single alphabet like a dictionary.

In comparison with the fully-indexed classified catalogue, the dictionary catalogue is simpler to use, the arrangement, easier to understand and is more particularly suited to quick reference under specific subjects than systematic perusal of subject representation in the library's stock.

In the dictionary catalogue, the primary or first line of arrangement is alphabetical. To meet the varying needs of readers, the catalogue has to provide more than one entry for a document. The alphabetical arrangement is found in:

1. Author catalogue
2. Name catalogue
3. Title catalogue
4. Subject catalogue
5. Dictionary catalogue
6. Alphabet-classed catalogue.

In these catalogues, the primary or first line of arrangement is alphabetical. Hence, the entries in a dictionary catalogue are arranged in one alphabet as follows:

Anup, Khan	(author)
Application of Computers	(title)
Art of Writing	(title)
Basu, Surana	(author)
Chakrabarthy, Visu	(author)
Cult of Vaishnavism	(subject)
Dutt, Toru	(author)
Dynasty of Mugals	(title)
Engineering	(subject)
Indian writing in English *see also* Dutt, Toru,	
Mugals *see also* Dynasty of Mugals (Reference)	
Ranganathan, S.R.	
Shakespeare, William	
World Wars.	

The dictionary catalogue is, therefore, a mixed variety—a combination of the author-title catalogue and the alphabetical subject catalogue. It is a "combination of two distinct and different approaches:

(a) The author or the title approach for those readers who know the book by its author or title only.

(b) The subject approach for those readers who do not know the book they want but require the material on some definite subject."

The dictionary catalogue is based on the principle of specific entry as far as subject entries are concerned. As the headings in a dictionary catalogue are arranged in one alphabet, the related subjects are often separated. It is one of the demerits of dictionary catalogue. For example, the words, 'Mugals' and 'Dynasty of Mugals' though related to each other are separated in the list stated above. Such related subjects, however can be united with one another by means of cross references known as

see and
see also

For example,

(a) Population
see
Demography

(b) Indian Industry
see also
Survey of Indian Industry

It is the responsibility of a cataloguer to select the subject headings carefully in order to be useful to the readers. As there is every chance of variation in the choice of subject headings it is advisable to go in for a standard book on subject headings. The following are the lists of standard universal subject headings:

1. Sear's list of subject headings.
2. The Library of Congress subject headings.
3. American Library Association list of subject headings.

Classified Catalogue

According to UNESCO's "Terminology of Documentation", classified catalogue is, "a catalogue arranged by subject according to a classification scheme".

It is a catalogue arranged by subject according to a systematic scheme of classification. In other words, the subject entries are arranged according to the call numbers and class numbers. Unlike other subject catalogues the entry headings are not verbal statements of subject but consist of notation symbols which represent subjects, forms and aspects and also convey the order of the schedules of the classification scheme adopted. The only demerit of the classified catalogue is that unless the user is fully conversant with the classification system, he would not be able to comprehend the sequence of entries.

The classified catalogue has got two parts, namely:

a. Classified part

b. Alphabetical part

In the classified catalogue, the subject entries are arranged according to the ordinal value of the symbols occupying the leading section of the entry in the language of the classification. It is known as the classified part. The other entries under author, title, collaborator series, etc. are arranged in an alphabetical sequence; it is known as alphabetical part.

Divided Catalogue

The divided catalogue is the catalogue of a single library or collection, which is separated into two or more sequences. The term is principally applied to a dictionary catalogue divided by the removal of subject and form entries together with their references, into an alphabetical subject catalogue and an author-title-series catalogue. In the divided catalogue the subject entries would be removed from the dictionary catalogue and filed separately. This results in two catalogues, namely, alphabetical author and title catalogue, and alphabetical subject catalogue. In other words, it has two or more sequences. For example:

(a) Two sequences: 1. Author, title; 2. Subject.

(b) Three sequences: 1. Author; 2. Title; 3. Subject.

Entries

The recording of a book in a catalogue under a suitable heading is known as an entry.

Headings are given for authors, subjects, titles, and references (see and see also) which are useful in identifying a book.

There are three kinds of entries in a catalogue. They are:

1. Main entry

2. Added entry
3. Reference entry.

Main Entry

Main entry is an entry which contains the maximum information required for the individualisation of a book. Main entries are prepared under the call number in a classified catalogue and under the author's surname in a dictionary catalogue.

Main entry is so called because it gives more information about the book than others. In a classified catalogue, the main entry is based on Classified Catalogue Code which is illustrated below:

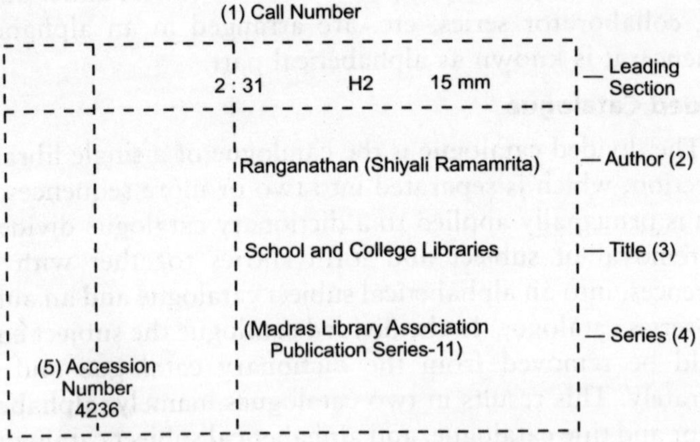

The function of this entry is to bring the book to the notice of the reader who remembers its subject matter only.

The main entry has got five sections. The first, or the leading section, is occupied by the call number of the book (2:31 H2).

The second section of a main entry gives the name of its author, the third gives its title, the fourth gives the series if any to which the book may belong. The fifth section invariably gives the accession number of the book.

Added Entry

Any entry other than main entry is called added entry. In cataloguing, it refers to secondary entry. An 'entry' other than the 'subject entry' and additional to the 'main entry' under which a bibliographical entity is represented in a catalogue is called the added entry.

It is the subsidiary entry under the joint authors, compilers, editor, translator, title, series or the subject of a book. Some of these are specific to the particular book, while some share with other books. The former are called specific added entries while the latter are called general added entries.

Reference Entry

The entry which guides the user from one heading to another is called reference entry. There are two kinds of reference entries. They are:

(a) See

(b) See also

The former is the simple direction from the heading not chosen in the catalogue to the one which has been chosen, e.g.,

Angling	Birds
see	see
Fishing	Aves.

The latter is a reference from an entry where the material is to be found in the subject catalogue to another, where other related materials can be located. The 'see also' references are usually given from the general subjects to the specific subjects, e.g.:

Carrot

see also

Vegetable

Analytical Entry

Analytical entry is an entry for a part of a document, including a reference to that document.

Normally we prepare cards for author, title and subject, but some valuable material hidden in the book may not ever see the light of the day. For example, a general book on Indian Economy may have a chapter on 'Five-Year Plans'. This chapter may be of immense use if it is filed with other entries on 'Five-Year Plans'—such an entry is called 'analytical entry'. This is supplementary to the comprehensive or main entry for the whole work.

It is an entry in a catalogue for part (forming part) of a book, periodical or other publication, article or contribution of separate authors in a collection (volume of essays, Festschrift, serial volume of musical compositions, etc.). The analytical entries may be made under authors, titles or subjects.

It is the analytical entry which describes a part of a work catalogued. In this respect, it differs from an added entry, which contains and covers whole of a work, e.g.:

ANALYTICAL ENTRY

Kumar (A)

History of Library Science education.

Forming Part of

John, Ed.: Curriculum of Library Science in Education

T: 2 (2) K4

The following is an illustration of entries and its subdivisions:

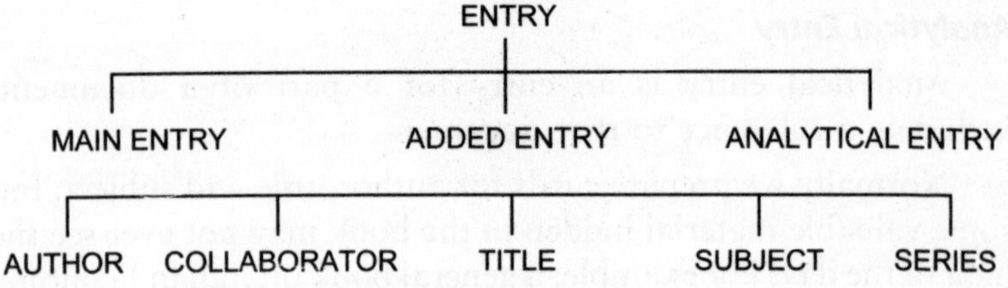

According to Dr. S.R. Ranganathan's 'Classified Catalogue Code' (CCC) a catalogue card should consist of the following sections:

1. Leading Section
2. Heading Section
3. Title Section
4. Note Section (Series and its editor, if any)
5. Accession Number Section, and
6. Tracing Section

Tracing Section

The other five sections have already been dealt with.

The 'tracing section' refers to an indication on the back of a main entry catalogue card showing under what added entries the book appears. In other words, it is an indication on the back of the main card of all added entries and references. A tracing section of classified catalogue is illustrated below:

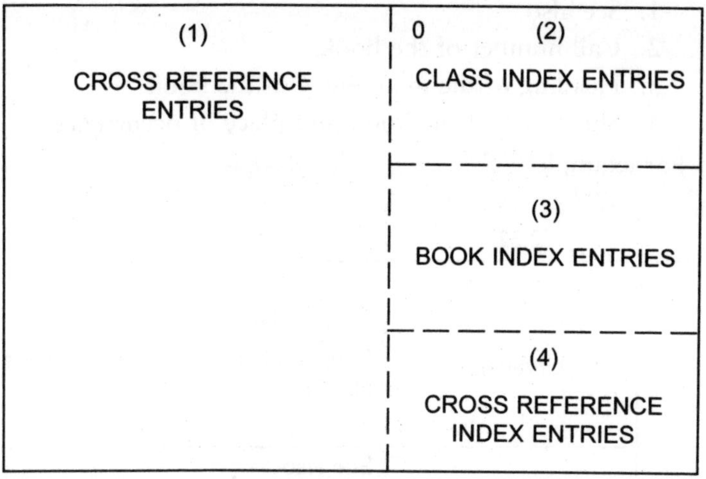

Fig. Tracing Section

The following are the sub-divisions of classified catalogue:

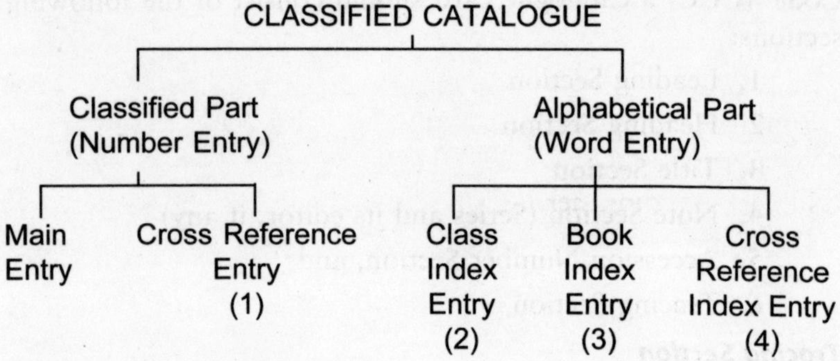

Cross Reference Entry

The 'cross reference entry' is a direction, from one of several headings under which an entry might be sought to the heading adopted, or to draw the attention to other headings under which related materials get entered. It is a specific subject entry which mentions a portion of a document in which the subject is treated, it is also known as 'subject analytical entry'. It consists of:

1. See also
2. Call number of the book
3. Heading of the main entry of the book
4. Short title of the book and place of occurrence

For example:

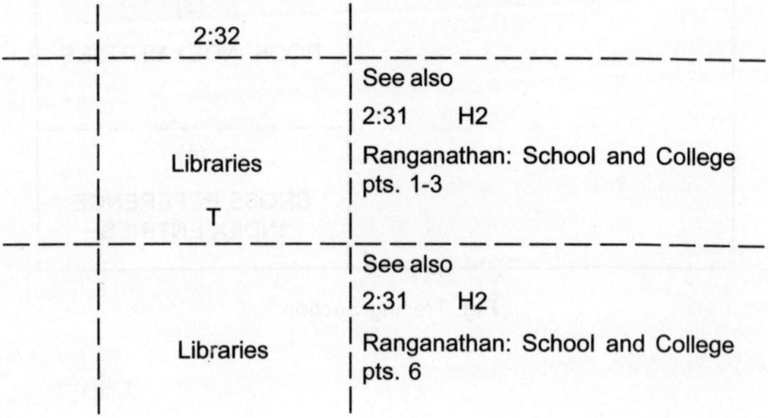

Class Index Entry

The function of the 'class index entry' is to direct the reader from the name of a subject to its class number, so that he may look up the appropriate region of the classified part of the catalogue, for the books the library has on that subject.

It is a general added word entry rendered under specific subject heading derived by chain procedure technique. The purpose of the class index entry in a classified catalogue is to act as an alphabetical index to its classified part.

Subject Heading

Subject heading is a word, term or a phrase chosen to express a concept or a concept combination in indexing and to constitute an entry.

There are several methods of deriving subject heading. The important among them are:

1. Subject Heading Lists
   (a) Sear's List
   (b) Library of Congress
2. Chain Procedure
3. Uniterm and Coordinating Indexing, etc.

Chain Procedure

The chain procedure is one of the important methods of deriving subject headings. It is based on the class number of the document.

According to the UNESCO's 'Terminology of Documentation' the chain procedure is, "a method of producing an alphabetical index of the term or phrases corresponding to the parts of a compound classified entry of a document where distributed relatives are displayed in relation to superior terms".

The class index entry headings are to be derived by chain procedure. The chain procedure is a semi-mechanical method for deriving subject heading from a class number.

The theory of chain procedure was first propounded by Dr. S.R. Ranganathan. According to him, the chain procedure is, "the standardised procedure whereby the successive terms in a chain of classes are transformed into heading for an alphabetical index".

The term 'chain' is the succession of divisions expressing the relation 'A includes B, which in turn includes C'. In other words, 'chain' means a series of successively subordinate terms.

The technique of constructing the index is that we have to take a class and start analysing it step by step. For example, the call number for the title 'William Shakespeare, the dramatist' is 0111, 2J64 (Shakespeare was born in 1564). For the above title, we can provide the chain procedure like this. First, we have to write the names of the subjects against the respective links. If a link ends with a connecting symbol, we have to write the word 'false link' against it. The numbers and words are to be connected by 'equal to' (=) sign. Then we have to join each link with the next succeeding link by a downward arrow.

We put the term 'sought link' against those links which represent subjects which are likely to be looked up by any reader seeking materials on the specific subject forming the last link of the full call number. Against other links we write the term 'unsought link'. Here is an example for the chain procedure:

0111, 2J64	=	William Shakespeare, the dramatist
0	=	Literature -> Sought Link
01	=	Unsought Link
011	=	Unsought Link
0111	=	English Literature -> Sought Link
0111,	=	False Link -> Unsought Link
0111, 2	=	English drama -> Sought Link
0111, 2J	=	Unsought Link
0111, 2J6	=	Unsought Link
0111, 2J64	=	Shakespeare's drama -> Sought Link

The number of 'class index entries' to be written for a class number are as many as the sought links present in the chain procedure representing the whole class number. In the above example, we have four class index entries. Write the class index entries starting from the lowest link and proceed upward. The term represented by the last digit of each of the 'sought links' is to be used as the class index entry heading. This term is to be taken from the schedule of classification.

In the added entry cards, every class index entry must be followed by a 'directing section'. It must be remembered that no full stop should be put at the end of the 'directing section'.

The following are the class index entries for the class number:

(1) SHAKESPEARE (WILLIAM), DRAMA

Directing Section — For document in this class and its Subdivisions see the Classified Part of the catalogue under the Class Number

0111,2J64

(2) ENGLISH, DRAMA

Directing Section — For document in this class and its Subdivisions see the Classified Part of the catalogue under the Class Number

0111,2J64

(3) LITERATURE

Directing Section — For document in this class and its Subdivisions see the Classified Part of the catalogue under the Class Number

0111,2J64

In the above example we have seen three links namely:

(1) Sought Links,

(2) Unsought Links, and

(3) False Links.

The Links

The links ending with a digit, representation of which provides such a heading which is quite likely to be looked for by the reader of the library, is known as a 'sought link'. In chain indexing, a step in notational hierarchy which is unwanted for indexing purposes is known as 'unsought link'.

In chain indexing, the false link refers to a step in the notational hierarchy where the notational chain gets lengthened by a symbol without an appropriate term being supplied in 'Colon Classification'. Here comma (,) is required to introduce personality facet which has no verbal equivalent, but being an indicator that a form is about to be employed. It usually represents relations between terms rather than concepts which are nameless.

Book Index Entries

It is the 'book index entry' which represents all the specific added entries. Its function is to bring the book to the notice of the reader who remembers only the name of its author, or any one of his collaborators, if any, or the series to which it may belong. In other words, it is the generic name used to denote the specific added word entries written for a classified catalogue. They belong to one or more of the following types:

(a) Author Index Entry

(b) Collaborator Index Entry

(c) Title Index Entry

(d) Series Index Entry.

The 'book index entry' must successively consist of the following sections:

1. Leading Section
2. Second Section
3. Index Number Section.

Examples of book index entries are given on next page 101.

Note

The following two points must be remembered. If there are two authors in the heading of a main entry, write another book index entry permuting the names present in it. Another important point is that the sub-title normally is omitted.

RANGANATHAN	(Shiyali Ramamrita)
	School and College Libraries
	2:31 H2

a. AUTHOR

DILLI KUMAR	(K.T.), Tr
	Ranganathan: School and College Libraries
	2:31 H2

b. COLLABORATOR

SCHOOL AND	COLLEGE LIBRARIES
	Ranganathan (Shiyali Ramamrita)
	2:31 H2

c. TITLE

Book Index Entries

Cross Reference Index Entry

It is a general added word entry referring from a heading to another heading, in other words, one word or set of words to another synonymous word in the alphabetical part.

According to Dr. S.R. Ranganathan, "It is another kind of general added entry. It directs the reader to the chosen name from any possible alternative name or from the name of the editor of a series to the name of the series."

The 'cross reference index entry' may be provided following categories:

1. For the alternative name
2. Editor of series
3. Generic name
4. Pseudonym—real name

5. Variant forms of name. It must consist of the following sections:
   (a) Leading Section (Referred from heading)
   (b) Second Section (See or see also)
   (c) Third Section (Referred to heading)

BALA BHASKAR (Prem)

See
PREM BALA BHASKAR

(a) ALTERNATIVE NAME

NEELAKANDAN (5). Ed.

See
MADRAS LIBRARY ASSOCIATION PUBLICATION SERIES

(b) EDITOR OF SERIES

EDUCATION CONFERENCE

See also
UNESCO INTERNATIONAL CONFERENCE OF EDUCATION

(c) GENERIC NAME

KALKI, PSEUD

See
KRISHNAMURTI (R)

(d) PSEUDONYM - REAL NAME

COLOR

See also
COLOUR

(e) VARIANT FORM

AACR-2 (1978)

AACR-2 defines a catalogue "as a list of library materials contained in a collection, a library or a group of libraries, arranged according to some definite plan". AACR-2 (1978) (Anglo-American Cataloguing Rules) edited by Michael Gorman and Paul W. Winkler has been jointly prepared by ALA (American Library Association), the British Library, Canadian Committee on Cataloguing, The Library Association (UK) and the Library of Congress (USA).

The introduction to this edition mentions that "it does not supersede the first edition (AACR-1; 1967) but continues it. The rules are still the Anglo-American Cataloguing Rules, having the same principles and underlying objectives as the first edition, and being firmly based on the achievements of those who created the work, first published in 1967."

AACR-2, which is a dictionary catalogue, has two parts:

Part I—Description

Part II—Heading, uniform titles and references.

The rules of Part I contain instructions as the formulation of descriptions of library materials. The rules in Part II are applicable to works and not generally to physical manifestation of those works, though the characteristics of an individual item are taken into account in some instances.

Physical Form of Catalogue

Though the rules in AACR-2 have been revised and augmented in the light of their application to mechanised cataloguing, they are equally suitable for any physical form of catalogue. The standard size of the card is 12.5 cm × 7.6 cm (approximately 5″ × 3″) with the thickness of 0.01 cm.

Description of Areas

The following eight areas normally identified in a book:

1. Title proper and statement of responsibility.
2. Edition statement.
3. Material (or type of publication)—specific details.
4. First publisher and date of publication.
5. Physical description.
6. Series.

7. Notes.
8. Standard number and terms of availability.

Main Entry of AACR-2

TA : 3 (2)		
NT3	Smith (John A)	
		Teaching of Library Science in University:
	An Indian view	of teaching library science/
	(by) John A. Smith—New Delhi: Sterling, 1973	
4562		XII, 160p.: 17cm (Library Science Series, No. 1)
		ISBN 0-7152
		1. Teaching Library Science | Title (Series)

Classified Catalogue Code Vs AACR

'Cataloguing' is the art of making records in such a manner that may be readily identified, located and examined. It is therefore, the most important reference tool designed for library users to facilitate identification and retrieval of documents by authors, title, subjects, series, etc. in the library. The purpose of catalogue is to put to order a collection of books so that the volumes may be located and used for reference and circulation. However, in meeting the above objectives a cataloguer may find problems cropping up in the form of complexities both in terms of the nature and types of materials available in libraries and in the form of subject, matter and authorship. This naturally paves the way for the refinement in the techniques of cataloguing code.

The following are widely used catalogue codes:

1. Ranganathan's Classified Catalogue Code (CCC)
2. Anglo-American Cataloguing Rules (AACR).

Ranganathan's Classified Catalogue Code is probably the first and the only Catalogue Code for the maintenance of Classified Catalogue. The rules have been guided by the Normative Principles.

The Anglo-American Cataloguing Rules was first published in 1967 and the second edition appeared in 1978. It is probably the most widely used Cataloguing Code in English speaking countries. The following are the major differences between the two codes:

CCC	AACR
1. It has been constructed for the maintenance of a classified catalogue.	1. It does not provide rules for subject cataloguing. It is a code primarily for author title cataloguing. It is used for dictionary catalogue.
2. It is meant for books and periodicals and provides rules for the author, title and subject. It provides rules for arrangement of entries also.	2. It is a comprehensive code for not only books and periodicals but also for non-book materials like microfilms, motion pictures and cartographic materials.
3. The CCC is based on a set of normative principles.	3. It is not based on any such principles.
4. Main entry heading must be in capital letters, e.g. SMITH (John).	4. Main entry is rendered in small letters, e.g. Smith (John).
5. In periodicals, the CCC calls for title proper (omitting the name of its sponsor).	5. The AACR, on the other hand, has retained the twin principles of author/title entry for periodicals also.
6. CCC generally advocates the removal of all honorifics.	6. The AACR suggests that honorifics, including certain titles be retained in certain cases.

CCC	AACR
7. The CCC does not make any provision for Indic names of persons.	7. The AACR approaches the problem of Indic names by classifying personal names by geographical area/language and provides rules for Indic names of person.
8. The CCC prescribes that the entry element in the subject heading for the administrative organ of the govt. is to be the word or word group denoting the sphere of work of the organ, e.g. India, Education (Ministry).	8. The AACR suggests that the name of organs be used as a subheading, e.g.: India, Ministry of Education.
9. The CCC is a selective catalogue, which contains selective information.	9. It is a descriptive catalogue containing all particulars of a book, author, title, imprint, collation, series, ISBN, etc.

Centralised Cataloguing

According to the "Terminology of Documentation" of UNESCO, Centralised Catalogue means, "the cataloguing by one library or cataloguing office within a system of libraries of all books acquired by all those libraries so that the results of such cataloguing are used by the individual libraries".

In other words, centralised cataloguing means that the books are not catalogued at the individual libraries to which they are allocated. It can be defined as "cataloguing of documents by some central organization".

Cataloguing is centralised so that all libraries under the system may get the benefit of it and thereby avoid duplication of same nature of work.

Objectives of Centralised Cataloguing

1. To avoid duplication of work.
2. To save time, money and wastage of human labour.
3. To achieve uniformity.
4. To enable member libraries provide better service to users.
5. To achieve better standards.

The centralised cataloguing may be done on either national or local level. The basic objective of centralised cataloguing is economy.

According to S.R. Ranganathan, if central cataloguing is implemented at the national level, there will be saving in the cost of cataloguing up to 79 per cent. If catalogue data is exchanged among countries there can be a similar saving at the international level. It is a general fact that in every library a considerable proportion of the total library expenditure (about 15% to 20%) is being spent on technical purposes.

Another advantage of central cataloguing is that it enables the libraries to make available books for consultation within a short time after acquisition by eliminating the delay in the technical processing of a book. In other words, the central agency which is responsible for central cataloguing, will be able to make available cataloguing data to individual libraries either along with the book or soon after its acquisition by the library.

Almost in all European countries the centralised cataloguing system is in vogue. The Library of Congress (LC) undertakes the task of centralised cataloguing and printing cards that any library may purchase. In addition to LC, some reputed companies are issuing printed cards of books published by them.

The novel system of centralised cataloguing is called MARC (Machine Readable Catalogue) which has been introduced by the Library of Congress in 1966. Through MARC, the LC records the cataloguing data on magnetic tape and supplies libraries with copies of the tapes.

Co-operative Cataloguing

According to "Terminology of Documentation" of UNESCO the term 'co-operative' means, "the sharing of common cataloguing operations by a number of libraries to avoid the duplication of effort".

In other words, co-operative cataloguing is the production of catalogue entries or printed book catalogues through the joint efforts of several independent libraries so that each library, and usually other non-co-operating libraries as well, may share the benefits of such cataloguing. Its objectives are to avoid duplication of effort by the co-operating libraries by the sharing of work and coverage of a wide-field of publications.

The term "co-operative cataloguing" is usually used to refer to a system where libraries produce catalogue data for their own stock and exchange this with catalogue data produced by other libraries. Thus cataloguing service is shared by several agencies for their mutual benefit. It is commonly associated with the maintenance of a Union Catalogue. The Shared Cataloguing Program of the Library Congress is an example of co-operative cataloguing in which catalogue entries prepared by various non-US national bibliographic agencies for publications of their respective countries are used by the LC with few modifications available to non-US publications for libraries in the US.

Co-operative cataloguing is a part of centralised cataloguing, if it is coordinated by a central agency which is responsible for distribution of the printed catalogue cards. The terms 'co-operative' and 'centralised' though seemingly closely related, are not strictly synonymous.

The advantages of co-operative cataloguing are as follows:

1. Saves wasteful duplication.
2. Better standard of cataloguing among participating libraries.
3. Uniformity of cards.
4. Saves the time of the readers in getting information, the available information among the participating libraries.
5. Easy to compile bibliography.

Arrangement of Entries

There are number of codes of rules for filing catalogue entries. The one which is mostly used is Classified Catalogue Code of Dr. S.R. Ranganathan, which is a complete catalogue code as far as books and periodicals are concerned. The CCC also provides rules for filing and arrangement of entries in the classified and alphabetical parts of catalogue.

Another code which has been brought out by the American Library Association (ALA) also provides a comprehensive code for alphabetisation of entries. It is widely used in libraries where a dictionary catalogue is in practice.

The rules for filing catalogue of ALA, may also be used for divided catalogue.

The classified catalogue has two parts, namely, alphabetical part and classified part. The classified part consists of number entries and the alphabetical part consists of word entries. Hence entries with a call number (class number and book number) are filed with classified part of a catalogue. The arrangement of class number therefore, depends on the ordinal values of the digits, constituting the call number. The CCC provides rules in this regard, which are as follows:

(a) The entries in the classified part are to be arranged by the class number in the leading section of the catalogue entries.

(b) A problem would arise, however, if two or more entries have the same class number within respective leading sections.

(c) If two or more entries have the same class number in their respective leading sections, entries with book numbers will have precedence over entries without book numbers, e.g.:

Alphabetisation of Entries

The arrangement of entries in the alphabetical part of classified catalogue or a dictionary catalogue can be broadly divided into two methods of alphabetisation. They are:

×	
	Kumar (Joy) Textbook of Economics
×	N3
	RAMAN (Lamba) Introduction to general Economics

1. word by word arrangement (known as 'nothing before something')
2. letter by letter arrangement (known as 'all through arrangement')

The above-mentioned arrangements are widely used in libraries. In the word by word arrangement, all the headings beginning with one word are arranged before those using the same letters to begin another word, whereas in the letter by letter arrangement, the letters in the heading would be arranged by letters only, whether they form a complete word or not. The following example would clear the meaning:

Word by word	**Letter by letter**
1. Call after	1. Call after
2. Call at	2. Call at
3. Call for	3. Called
4. Call girl	4. Call for
5. Call off	5. Call girl
6. Call on	6. Calling
7. Called	7. Call off
8. Calling	8. Call on

According to Dr. S.R. Ranganathan, the general rule is that entries should be arranged strictly by the alphabets. According to the ALA Rules which is intended for a dictionary catalogue—all entries both English and foreign are arranged alphabetically according to the order of the English alphabet. The arrangement is to be word by word.

With the introduction of electronic gadgets in the field of information, the art of cataloguing has evolved many changes. The manual searching of entries have been replaced by machine searching. In other words, the Machine Readable Catalogue (MARC) has come in vogue in the field of library science. The MARC has been designed as a means of quickly disseminating cataloguing information in a form suited to the various needs of libraries. It also has the facility of on-line computer system.

Information Sources

8

According to 'Terminology of Documentation' of UNESCO, an information source means, 'the source from which an individual gets information to fulfil his needs'. It is a general fact that the foundation of any discipline is its literature.

It is true that if any one wishes to advance his knowledge in a chosen area, he has to invariably look into the records and experiences left by his predecessors. In olden days only documents like books and periodicals constituted the collection of a library. But the modern library is being redesignated as an information centre. Naturally the collection is in tune with the information technology. Besides books and periodicals, the unpublished documents have also become a vital information source.

Types of Information Sources

The information sources may be broadly divided into two, namely:

(a) Documentary sources

(b) Non-documentary sources.

The documentary sources are sub-divided into three types:

(i) Primary sources

(ii) Secondary sources

(iii) Tertiary sources.

Primary Sources

According to UNESCO's 'Terminology of Documentation', primary sources are 'fundamental authoritative material relating to a subject, used in the preparation of other written work'. In other words, the primary sources are original manuscripts, contemporary records or documents which are used by an author in writing a book or other literary compilation.

These are the first-hand material, which have not been filtered through interpretation and are the first published records of original research and development. Most of the primary sources are accounts of experiments with findings and conclusions, like laboratory notebooks, diaries, research reports and correspondences.

The following are the materials of primary sources:

1. Periodicals (report on discovery/original thinking)
2. Research reports
3. Seminar/conference proceedings
4. Scientific reports
5. Government's official publications
6. Patents (Indian patents office)
7. Standards (ISI)
8. Theses and dissertations.

Secondary Sources

Secondary sources of information are those which are either compiled from or refer to primary sources of information. They are documents containing data or information about 'primary documents'.

The primary sources are rather unorganised sources, which are difficult to use as such. The secondary sources help us to use them. In other words, the original information is modified and reorganised to suit the information needs of the users. The primary sources normally are circulated to private and limited users only. The secondary sources, which satisfy the information needs of the potential users by appearing in normal form, are widely circulated.

Hence the secondary sources are repacked knowledge rather than new knowledge. They serve not only the purpose of disgested information but also as bibliographical key to the primary sources.

The secondary sources too are published, like the primary sources, in the following forms:

1. Periodicals (summaries of findings)
2. Indexing and Abstracting periodicals
3. Review of progress
4. Reference books:
   (a) Encyclopaedias
   (b) Dictionaries
   (c) Handbooks
   (d) Treatises
   (e) Textbooks
5. Translation.

Tertiary Sources

Tertiary sources are the reading materials which are condensed and distilled from the primary and the secondary sources. The main function of the tertiary sources is to assist the searcher of information in the use of primary and secondary sources. These sources normally do not contain subject knowledge. These too are published in the following variety of forms:

1. Year books
2. Directories
3. Bibliographies
4. Guides to literature
5. Bibliography of bibliographies.

Non-documentary Sources

Non-documentary sources of information form a major part of communication exclusively in the field of science and technology. There are two kinds of non-documentary sources:

1. Formal, and
2. Informal.

The formal sources include universities, consultants, industries, research institutions and government departments. The informal sources comprise of conversation with colleges, visitors, attendance at professional meetings, etc. The informal sources are rather live sources, which are very important in the process of communication.

The informal sources are considered to be more convenient and easily accessible because in such cases exchange of information occurs between two experts, so they help each other in getting right information at the right time, instead of wasting time in seeking information from the documentary sources.

It is generally believed that the primary sources are more up-to-date than the rest of the sources. A researcher usually starts his search with the secondary and the tertiary sources and ends up the search with the primary sources.

Uses of Information Sources

The sources of information, whether they are primary, secondary, tertiary or non-documentary sources, are of immense use to the different types of users. The following are the benefits of such sources:

1. To keep abreast of the latest information in relevant areas.
2. To avoid duplication of research in the same area.
3. To enable the researcher in getting more information in his chosen area.
4. To furnish background information to understand a subject, new or unfamiliar.
5. To supply necessary answers to specific queries.
6. To offer a fruitful path of information.

Bibliographies

The term 'Bibliography' has been derived from the Greek terms, 'Biblion' and 'Graphien'. 'Biblion' means 'books' and 'Graphien' means 'to write'. Hence, etymologically, bibliography means the writing of books.

The term bibliography is rather a complicated one, largely because different terms have been used by different people for the same kind of bibliography. Here are a few definitions of bibliography:

Bibliography is a list of books and sometimes of other material such as periodicals, articles and illustrations, written by one author, or on one subject. It is the art of correctly describing books, loosely, the science of books.

According to Esdaile, bibliography is the art of recording books, the science of making of books and of their extent record. It is a list of books arranged according to some permanent principle—an annotated catalogue of documents. In other words, it is the technique of compiling systematically descriptive lists of manuscripts or published records of different kinds which are not in the possession of one library or owner. It is rather a printed list of documents containing formal descriptions of the documents.

The term bibliography as the science of books has wider implications. It includes not only the technique of book-building but also the history of books and their changing forms, method of printing, etc.

The terms 'Bibliography' and 'Catalogue' seem to have related functions, but they differ in their characteristics. A bibliography is an organised list of documents and is not limited to collection of a particular library, whereas a library catalogue is a list of documents contained in a library.

Types of Bibliographies

Diversity of purpose or variety of interests is the basis for the production, as well as the classification of bibliographies into various types. The bibliographies may be broadly divided into three types:

1. Systematic or enumerative,
2. Analytical or critical, and
3. Historical.

Systematic or Enumerative Bibliographies

Systematic bibliography is a bibliography which is arranged according to a classification scheme. It is nothing but a straightforward listing of books and other reading materials according to some useful method for study and reference. The basic purpose of systematic bibliography is to collate and list information about individual books and related materials in a logical order.

The systematic bibliography is divided in different ways by library professionals and experts like Arundell Esdaile, Van Hoeson and S.R. Ranganathan.

It was Arundell Esdaile who has divided the bibliography into two broad groups, namely, primary and secondary. Further these are sub-divided into the following types:

Primary Bibliographies

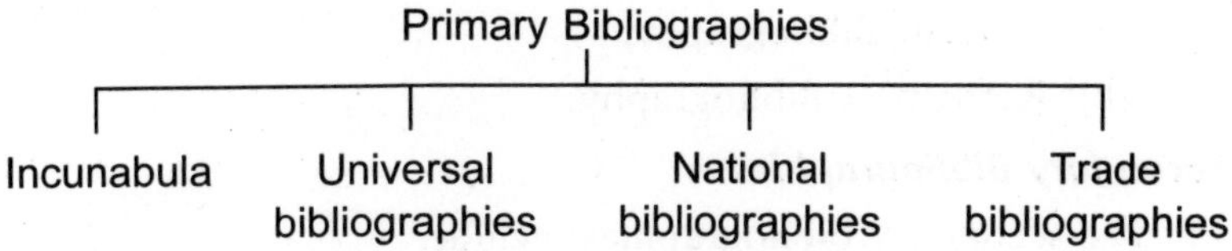

1. Incunabula or book rarities bibliographies include material available up to the 15th century. These are valuable because they include rare material restricted to that period only, e.g. Index to the early printed books in the British Museum.

2. The universal bibliography is a comprehensive bibliography and not limited by time, place, language, subject and author. It is a list of all documents of all forms of materials, produced in all countries, e.g.:

(i) International Catalogue of Scientific Literature.

(ii) International Federation of Library Association (IFLA).

(iii) UNESCO.

3. National bibliography includes almost all the books produced in a country. Each entry furnishes bibliographical information such as author, title, imprint and collection. The geographical fact is the controlling factor in this type. It is almost a complete record of printed output in a given country, e.g.:

(i) Indian National Bibliography.

(ii) British National Bibliography.

4. Trade bibliography is a list of books or other reading materials available for sale. These are brought out by commercial organizations like publishers, printers, etc., e.g.:

(i) Books in Print.

(ii) Government Books in Print.

The trade bibliographies normally provide minimum bibliographic details of the documents listed but they give the prices which are not generally given in other types of bibliographies. These bibliographies can be distinguished into two types:

(a) Current Bibliography.

(b) Retrospect Bibliography.

Secondary Bibliographies

The secondary bibliographies include:

(i) Elective or Selective Bibliographies.

(ii) Subject Bibliographies.

(iii) Bibliography of Bibliographies.

(i) The elective or selective bibliography lists the best or selected books, for a certain type of library or a reader. It may be current or retrospective. This is the best tool for the selection of material, e.g.:

(a) Standard catalogue of public libraries.

(b) Sonnenschein, W.S. Best books.

(ii) The subject bibliography is a comprehensive list of material on a given subject. The subject may be a person, place or a topic. To S.R. Ranganathan, the subject bibliography is a document bibliography confined to a specific subject field only, instead of covering the entire universe of subject, e.g.:

(a) Bibliography on Mahatma Gandhi.

(b) The Oxford Bibliography of Indian History.

(iii) As there are many types of bibliographies on various subjects, it is necessary that they must be controlled for the benefit of users. Thus, the bibliography of bibliographies is primarily a list of bibliographies, recording in some logical arrangement all bibliographies.

According to Dr. S.R. Ranganathan, bibliographies may be classified according to the following three ways:

1. Based on the three characteristics of a book (atma, suksham and sthaula).
2. Based on the five fundamental categories (PMEST).
3. Based on the 'economic—bibliographical chain' (producer, distributor and consumer).

Analytical or Critical Bibliography

An analytical bibliography involves 'investigation of the physical nature of the book which can be and frequently has been sufficiently exhaustive to make all the circumstances of the book's manufacture and history to be revealed'. The analytical bibliography has an important relationship to descriptive cataloguing and the history of the book.

Historical Bibliography

The study of books 'as objects of art' is termed as historical bibliography. It is concerned with the art of writing, illumination and finding.

The historical bibliography makes an attempt to achieve a broad understanding of milieu of the books in the context of the world of books and social and cultural conditions existing at the time.

Uses of Bibliographies

The bibliographies are important and useful sources for promotion of research and development. They are the essential tools for the reference librarian to help him give the right information at the right time to the right researcher.

The following are the uses of bibliographies:

1. It is true that volumes of books are being published every day and the librarian cannot buy all the books. Through bibliographies, he selects books for his library.

2. It saves the time of the readers, by providing them with a host of list of books in a chosen area. The reader, without wasting his time, gets benefited by bibliographies.
3. It serves as a guide to the literature of a subject.
4. It also helps in the preparation of new bibliographies.
5. It helps in giving the literary output of a nation for a particular year (INB, BNB).
6. It assists in promoting useful applications of existing knowledge and in making the applications which have been developed in one country widely known to all countries (UNESCO).
7. It promotes the effectiveness of particular projects in research (UNESCO).

Information Services

9

The word 'information' is a complex term and it is extremely difficult to define it precisely. According to 'Terminology of Documentation' of UNESCO, the term 'information' means 'a message used to represent a fact or concept by the unity of a data medium and its meaning'.

Information is knowledge put to use, which may produce good or bad effects. It is the product of human brain in action. It remains as one of the essential components of good communication process. A piece of information is not any individual's, but a national resource. It becomes common property resulting in an increased usage of information. More the utilisation, more is the production of information.

Need for Information Centre

In our rapidly changing society, difficulty in obtaining and exploiting information is increasing. It is true that the information gap between the source of information and the recipient has been widened. At one end is the complex universe of information and at the other end, is the population of users—various needs, requirements. These two elements are to be bridged and interlinked. Here, information centre comes in handy. It acts as an agent of information transfer by streamlining the available right information to the right users at the right time.

Hence, any centre which acquires, organises and distributes information to the user community is termed as 'information centre'. Thus an information centre is an 'organization of people, materials and machines that serve to facilitate the transfer of information from one person to another'.

Need for Information Service

According to 'Terminology of Documentation' of UNESCO, information service is defined as 'a service aiming at the actual information of its users'. In other words, it is a service provided to an individual or institutions by an information centre, which draws attention to information possessed in its department in anticipation.

It is a general notion among the users that libraries offer no other service other than lending books for reading at home. Libraries offer rather a wide range of services, viz.:

1. Books from its own collection for reading at home.
2. Books from other libraries by way of inter-library loan for use in study and research.
3. Assistance in the use of catalogue and classification system of the library.
4. Assistance in the use of reference books.
5. Preparation of bibliographies.
6. Assistance to use audio-visual resources.
7. Providing documentation services such as translation, indexing, abstracting and photocopying.
8. Extension services.

The library services may broadly be divided into two, namely:

(a) Reader services, and
(b) Auxiliary services.

The reader's services include charging and discharging, inter-library loan, reference services, etc. The auxiliary services comprise documentation—translation, indexing, abstracting, photocopying, audio-visual and extension services.

The factors which influence the need for information service are categorised as follows:

1. Growth of literature (information explosion).
2. Different forms of publication (traditional books, modern-micro forms).

3. Language of publication.
4. Escalating prices of documents.
5. Growth of user population.
6. Information awareness.
7. Forms of communication (formal and informal).
8. Communication barriers (time, cost, geography/distance, etc.).

Reference Service

The information centre is charged with the responsibility of collecting, preserving, organising and distributing of information. Unless the librarians make publicity of the services available in their libraries, the users will not benefit much from them.

The dissemination of information is the basic objective of any information centre. And it can only be achieved by establishing a contact with the users. This kind of service—in action—is generally known as 'Reference Service'. In other words, the reference service is the personalised assistance rendered by the library staff to the users in finding an information regarding their study and research.

In modern special libraries, this service is also known as 'Information Service'. This service ranges from helping users in finding simple facts, tracing books, keeping users informed of current literature in specialised subject fields and finding specialised information. The object of reference service is to assist readers on all levels by serving as guide, interpreter and information agency.

According to Dr. S.R. Ranganathan, Reference Service is, "the process of establishing right contact between the right reader and the right book at the right time and in the right personal way. It is a personal service to each reader in helping him to find the documents answering his interest at the moment, pin-pointedly, exhaustively and expeditiously." According to Louis Shores, 'Reference is to information service what intelligence is to military.'

It was Louis Shores who chalked out the reference service work which includes:

1. Supervision.
2. Information.
3. Guidance.
4. Instruction.
5. Bibliography.
6. Appraisal.

It was Dr. S.R. Ranganathan who on the basis of time factor distinguished two different aspects of reference service. They are:

(i) Ready reference service, and

(ii) Long range reference service.

Ready Reference Service

The Ready reference service refers to a reference work which is concerned with questions of a factual nature which can be answered readily, generally from quick reference books which in many libraries have been shelved together with standard reference books.

To Ranganathan, the ready reference service is more or less fact finding service which normally consumes not more than five minutes. Hence, the concept of ready reference service is based on the duration of time taken. As this service involves a very short time, it is also known as fact finding service or short range reference service. For example, questions like:

(a) What does UNESCO stand for?

(b) What is the name of instrument which measures earthquakes?

can be answered in a minute or two. The answers to these questions can be provided by ready reference service since they normally involve short time and can be answered by referring to the books available in a library such as the:

Dictionaries

Encyclopaedias

Directories

Year Books

Handbooks

Biographical sources

Bibliographies.

These reference sources should be supplemented by the files and records maintained in the reference section. It is true that the success of ready reference service largely depends upon the ability of the reference staff.

Long Range Reference Service

Long range reference service is rather a new phenomenon and an offshoot of special library service. As implied by its very name, there can be no question of giving immediate response in long range reference service. The long range reference service normally takes longer time. This is mainly due to the following three influencing factors:

1. Time involved
2. Sources of information
3. The nature of information sought.

In the long range reference service, immediate satisfaction cannot be provided. As it involves time, the exact time factor cannot be ascertained. While referring about the long range reference service, Dr. S.R. Ranganathan says, "Few long-range reference questions take less than half-an-hour, while some may take a whole day or even weeks."

The sources of information as far as the ready reference service is concerned are restricted to reference books like dictionaries, encyclopaedias, year books, directories, etc. But in the long range reference service, the search starts with the sources of ready reference and is continued into books, periodicals, informal sources, non-book materials, etc. The search may continue by taking help from other libraries—national or international. Besides, the reference librarian must be a capable person. He should know the development and trends in the universe of knowledge.

In the ready reference service, the nature of information is concerned with facts. On the other hand, the long range reference service is concerned with a prolonged search where the factual information has no value. In other words, the information sought may involve exposition of a problem from a particular point of view, e.g. 'the role of Centre in eradicating illiteracy', 'World Bank's assistance to promote water bases', etc.

The following is the nature of information as far as long range reference services are concerned:

1. The information sought may be too specialised, e.g. information seeking behaviour of researchers in economics.
2. The information sought may involve an opinion on a particular idea, e.g. the role of cinema in escalating crimes.
3. The information sought may be too recent and could be available only in recent newspapers and periodicals, e.g. the reservation policy.
4. The information sought might be available in foreign language and it requires translation service.
5. The information sought might have appeared in a journal not available in the library. The same may be borrowed by inter-library loan.

For the long range reference service to be successful, it is essential that the reference librarian possess good mastery of bibliographical organization and also familiarity with growth and development of the universe of subjects.

Documentation

According to UNESCO's 'Terminology of Documentation', the term 'Documentation' is 'the continuous and systematic processing of documents or data. It includes location, identification, acquisition, analysis, storage, retrieval, circulation and preservation for the specialised information of users. In other words, documentation refers to the act of collecting, classifying and making readily accessible the records of all kinds of intellectual activity.'

Documentation also refers to the recording of knowledge and the sources of knowledge, organising such records systematically so that they may be found quickly, and disseminating by various means both the knowledge and the sources of the knowledge. It includes the activities which constitute special librarianship plus the prior activities of preparing and reproducing materials and the subsequent activity of distribution.

According to Dr. S.R. Ranganathan, the word 'Document' means "embodied thought—a record of work on paper or other material, for easy physical handling, transport across space, and preservation through time".

It was ASLIB who adopted the definition of the term 'documentation' for the 'Journal of Documentation' in 1945 as "recording, organization and dissemination of specialised knowledge". According to Dr. S.R. Ranganathan, documentation is the promotion and practice of bringing into use nascent micro-thought by specialists.

The following are the five facets of documentation:

1. Documentation work,
2. Documentation service,
3. Abstracting work,
4. Documentation reproduction service, and
5. Translation service.

Documentation Centre

'Documentation Centre' is an organization primarily limited to selecting, acquiring, storing and retrieving specific documents, disseminating them only in response to requests expressed as unique numbers. Traditionally, libraries have been performing the three basic functions, viz., collection, storage and provision of documents. It is true that the traditional library tools and services have proved to be ineffective in the context of provision of specialised and intensified service to specialists. The shifting emphasis is towards the dissemination of specific information contained in documents, rather than the documents themselves. This has resulted in the emergence of 'Documentation Centres' to achieve the purpose of providing intensified documentation service.

The following are the few documentation centres of India:

1. Indian National Scientific Documentation Centre (INSDOC)
2. Indian Council of Agricultural Research (ICAR)
3. Council of Scientific and Industrial Research (CSIR)
4. Indian Council of Medical Research (ICMR)
5. Social Science Documentation Centre (SSDC)
6. Defence Science Information Documentation Centre (DESIDOC)
7. National Information System for Science and Technology (NISSAT)
8. Small Enterprises National Documentation Centre (SENDOC)
9. Indian Council of Social Science Research (ICSSR).

INSDOC

INSDOC was set up in 1952 with the technical assistance from UNESCO. In 1964, UNESCO assisted INSDOC in setting up its regional centre in Bangalore. It is functioning under the Council of Scientific and Industrial Research.

The organizational structure of INSDOC comprises of the following sections:

(a) Documentation Service Section
(b) Translation Section
(c) Documentation Work Section
(d) Printing Section
(e) Photo Reproduction Section
(f) Administration Section.

The following are the services rendered to the information seekers:

(i) It supplies copies of scientific papers in the form of microfilm and photocopies.
(ii) It serves even by getting copies from foreign documentation centres.

(iii) It helps in translating foreign scientific papers to English (The service is offered in translation of eighteen foreign languages to English).

(iv) It prepares Bibliography on requests and compiles a list of references to recent papers on any specified scientific subject.

(v) It also undertakes technical enquiries of fact-finding nature.

(vi) It offers selective dissemination of information services also (SDI).

SENDOC

SENDOC was set up in 1971 at the SIET (Small Industry Extension Training) Institute to cater to the information needs of the small-scale sector entrepreneurs development and promotional agents, training and consultancy organization.

The following are the objectives of SENDOC:

1. To collect, process and store information data and documents useful for the technical and managerial advancement of small industries.
2. To be a national centre for co-ordinating and collaborating—liasion with similar centres in other countries.

NISSAT

In 'Science and Technology Plan Seminar' in 1973, plans for improvement of information facilities in our country were discussed. And it directly paved way for the establishment of NISSAT. It was established in 1977 by the Government of India, under the Department of Science and Technology (DST).

Objectives

1. To cooperate with different scientific and technical agencies in the country.

2. To evolve 'national standards', compatible with international standards and to co-ordinate with international information system.

3. To conduct symposium, seminars and workshops to promote training and education of information scientists.

4. To see that at least one useful scientific publication is available in the country.

5. To provide on-line and computerised SDI services.

Documentation Services

The twentieth century has been witnessing an enormous growth of literature in the form of macro and micro documents. In order to meet the challenge of knowledge explosion, the library profession has come forward to share the responsibility of making available the information needs of the scientists and researchers in their chosen areas. It is true that with the traditional methods of librarianship the librarians cannot serve them well. Hence, they have opted for the new technique which involves providing up-to-date information on micro thought, pin-pointedly and exhaustively to the scientific researcher and scholar. This is known as 'Documentation'.

To meet the current information needs of the users, organization of documentation service has become an essential prerequisite in modern libraries. As a result, specialised documentation centres have also come up to act as clearing house for specialised information. The documentation service comprises of the following services:

1. Current Awareness Service (CAS)
2. Selective Dissemination of Information (SDI)
3. Indexing and abstracting services
4. Translation services
5. Bibliographic services
6. Reprographic services.

Current Awareness Service (CAS)

A current awareness service is 'a service which provides users with the latest information, or published literature, on their particular subject of interest'. Current awareness may be defined as 'knowledge of recent developments'. The main aim of this service is to alert users for the new publications. These are generally selective, and some special libraries bring out the contents of the latest issues of the periodicals and circulate them among the users privately.

The lists of monthly new additions brought out by different libraries also serve a similar purpose. As research activities in many fields in India depend upon the information sources of Western origin which normally take a considerable time in reaching them, the current awareness service is found very effective for the dissemination of latest nascent information.

The current awareness involves a knowledge of:

(a) new theoretical ideas and hypothesis,

(b) new problems to be solved,

(c) new methods and techniques for solving,

(d) new and old problems, and

(e) new circumstances affecting what people do and how they do it.

Hence, a current awareness service is a device of the information centre through which the users of information can be informed promptly after the publication, but before absorption into the comprehensive secondary sources of current literature on a broad subject field.

Selective Dissemination of Information (SDI)

Selective dissemination of information is a service which continually disseminates documents, references, abstracts or data selected according to the interest profiles of the users. The SDI is a current awareness service geared towards the individuals, unlike CAS which is meant for groups. It is also known as 'personalised service'.

The CAS tailored to the interests of individual scientists and research scholars are a recent innovation which the computer has made possible. The processes involved in production of such personalised bibliographies are generally referred to as SDI system.

The SDI has become the most advanced machine based information service. Progress has been rapid because SDI systems handle relatively small volumes of citations and also because they are able to rely on a continuous stream of new input data for some years now.

Indexing and Abstracting Services

'Indexing' is an assignment of index terms to documents or objects with the aim to be able later on to retrieve the documents or objects according to the selected concepts designated by the index terms. In other words, indexing is a method which is used to retrieve information from a table in memory or a file on a direct access store.

Abstracting refers to a form of current bibliography in which sometimes books, but mainly contributions to periodicals, are summarized. They are accompanied by adequate bibliographical descriptions to enable the publications or articles to be traced, and are frequently arranged in classified order. They may be in their original language or translated into English or some other language. Periodicals which contain only abstracts are known as journals of abstracts or abstract journals.

Abstracting is usually non-critical indication of the subject contents of a document, aiming to permit the user to make a decision about the relevance of the document. In order to keep scientists and research scholars informed of the current publications, many libraries and specialised agencies bring out the indexes and abstracts. An index provides clue to the location of the information in general or on a specialised subject. It generally contains the author, title, name of the host document with the bibliographical details like the volume number, data and pages, whereas an abstract provides the summary of the thought contents of the articles, in addition to the index information.

The process of preparing the indexes and abstracts oriented to special needs of the users are referred to as Indexing and Abstracting services. These are an important part of the documentation service. The following are the few examples of indexes and abstracts available in India.

Indexes

1. Index India
2. Guide to Indian Periodical Literature (Social Science and Humanities)

3. Indian Science Index
4. The Indian Press Index.

Abstracts

1. ICSSR Research Abstracts
2. Indian Behavioural Science Abstracts
3. Indian Dissertation Abstracts
4. Indian Library Science Abstracts
5. Indian Science Abstracts.

Translation Services

It is estimated that presently there are 3000 languages in the world. Out of these we have more than 50 million people speaking just 13 languages. These are English, Chinese, Hindi, Spanish, Russian, German, Japanese, Indonesian, French, Italian, Portuguese, Arabic and Bengali. Around 47 per cent of the literary output is brought out in English. And 35 per cent literary output is brought out in Russian, French and German. Moreover all the primary sources are brought out only in English, Russian, French and German.

The above survey would drive home the point that unless we have translation facilities we may not get the relevant information required for the researchers. Hence, the translation service has become an integral part of the documentation services. INSDOC has taken the job of translating important documents published in languages other than English.

It is estimated that 50 per cent of the literature in Science and Technology is published in languages other than English. Scientists, researchers and scholars not familiar with those languages would be deprived of using the respective literature in those languages and *vice versa*. The solution to this problem is Translation service.

National documentation centres and translation agencies employ a number of translators in different languages and also maintain a panel of translators whose services may be utilised whenever needed. In this context, National Library of India has published 'Index Translationum Indicarum', a collection of about

2,800 translations published in India. Entries are arranged by Indian languages and then by authors in an alphabetical order. The index gives author of the original, title of translation, name of translator, and other bibliographical details.

Bibliographic Services

For purposeful and planned reading on a subject, it is necessary to prepare a bibliography, without which it would be difficult for the advanced students, researchers, to do research on a subject or a project. It is often said to be the first task in a research study. Hence, the library and the information centres offer a wide range of bibliographic services, by preparing bibliography on a particular subject or topic on request.

The bibliographic services can be offered at three levels, namely, national, regional and international. The pattern of bibliographic services in India may be recognised better from the point of view of the national organization, programmes and activities. For example, the National Library has undertaken the task of compilation of national bibliography. Besides, INSDOC compiles a list of references to recent papers on any specified scientific subject on request.

The following national information centres too, offer bibliographic services:

(a) ICSSR (Indian Council of Social Science Research)

(b) SENDOC (Small Enterprises National Documentation Centre)

(c) BARC (Bhaba Atomic Research Centre)

(d) ICAR (Indian Council of Agricultural Research).

Reprographic Services

According to UNESCO's 'Terminology of Documentation' the word Reprography is, "the whole set of copying and micro-copying processes using all forms of radiation, all duplicating and office printing processes including ancillary operations connected with such processes".

The reprographic service is also known as copying service. If any document is of rare nature, it cannot be loaned out. The work of the user may either be held up or suffer from want of desired document. Under such situations, a reprographic of the document would serve the purpose of the user. The greatest use made of reprography is in getting copies of texts, charts, etc. from other libraries—national and international. The well-known method of photocopying is xeroxing. It is in vogue in almost all libraries.

The following are the reasons for the increase in demand for reprographic services:

(a) The phenomenon of scatter of literature.
(b) The lack of self-sufficiency of any information centre.
(c) The hike in the cost of journal subscriptions.
(d) To facilitate and promote inter-library service.
(e) Majority of research scholars prefer to possess copies of essential literature of their interest.
(f) The economic factor.

Reprographic Services in India

It was M.C. Trivedi who highlighted the potentialities of reprography in India. The Indian National Scientific Documentation Centre set up in 1952 under CSIR started a systematic reprographic service in the year of its establishment. It was assisted by the UNESCO by way of equipping all the infrastructure facilities. The regional centres of INSDOC too started reprographic services.

On request, INSDOC provides copies of scientific papers of the library resources available within India and as a last resort from foreign centres on reciprocal arrangements. It charges a nominal fee for the service. The following information centres too offer reprographic services:

(a) National Archives of India
(b) BARC
(c) ICAR
(d) CSIR
(e) NISSAT

Reprographic is communication, not production. It is one of the fastest growing technologies. Making of a single copy for the purpose of research or private study is not an infringement of copyright laws. Copying by libraries (non-profit making) is permitted for an individual.

Application of Computers in Libraries

10

India has made great strides in computer and telecommunication technologies. It was one of the first few nations which realised the potentialities of computers for bibliographical information work and routine library house-keeping operations.

Computer is one of the most powerful tools ever designed by man to solve problems that involve computing and processing of data. It can manipulate and transform all kinds of data at a tremendously fast speed without a mistake. It has no brain, therefore, it has to be instructed to perform a task and supplied with necessary information in the most detailed form in a language which it can understand. The solution to the problem may be expressed first diagrammatically using flowcharts and then written in a computer programming language.

Automation

According to Webster's Dictionary, automation is, "the technique of making an apparatus, a process or a system operate automatically". In other words, it is the machinery that mathematically manipulates information storing, selects, presents and records input data or internally generated data.

Mechanisation of library house-keeping operations predominantly by computers is known as library automation. The term 'library automation' is used extensively to refer to the use of computers to perform some of the traditional activities such as:

(a) acquisition,

(b) serial control,

(c) cataloguing,
(d) circulation.

and some related fields such as:

(a) information retrieval,
(b) automatic indexing,
(c) abstracting,
(d) automatic textual analysis, and
(e) resource sharing through networks.

Need for Automation

On account of information and knowledge explosion, it has become essential for librarians to provide a master key to this repository of knowledge. To make the maximum use of this tremendous upsurge of knowledge in the service of humanity, the librarians started mechanising activities of libraries and research institutions through various gadgets.

New techniques have entered into the field of library and as a result the librarians are expected to serve computerized on-line services, SDI and CAS services to the users. The following are the needs for computerisation of library activities:

(a) Information explosion (Growth of documents)
(b) New techniques
(c) Depth of content analysis—selection and manipulation
(d) Immediate access to specialised information (It is considered as a spring board to the researchers)
(e) Users' services (Heavy influx of documents added new dimensions to users' needs)
(f) Greater efficiency
(g) Economy in human labour, money and time
(h) Accuracy and promptness in service
(i) Availability of information in machine readable form
(j) Elimination of duplication of work
(k) Large data can be handled with ease and accuracy

(l) To share the resource sharing among different libraries (through computer networks—nationally and internally).

Benefits of Computers in Library

According to J.H. Sharma, "Automation helps in solving the problem of staff shortage, reduces mistakes, quality of tasks is better and economy in time is achieved."

The computer application in bibliographical information handling has manifold advantages. Firstly, routine and repetitive jobs are handled with ease thereby saving labour and eliminating drudgery. In a mechanised system, there can be only one input for many different operations and outputs.

The second advantage is speed and the third benefit is productivity is improved. Computer application is able to restructure work, redefine jobs and in the process re-allocate resources. Fourthly, it contributes to efficiency in terms of recall and precision parameters. The following are the benefits of computers in libraries:

(a) Solution to staff shortage and reduction in mistakes
(b) Higher rate and better quality of tasks
(c) Reduction in time
(d) Saving in cost in personnel and cost effective
(e) Better control over records, they can be kept up-to-date
(f) Eliminates duplication of work
(g) Large data can be handled with ease and accuracy
(h) Automation is very economic if a large quantity of information is to be manipulated.

Automation
- (1) Easy Functioning
- (2) Accuracy
- (3) Economy in human labour, money and time
- (4) Promptness in service

Computer Application in Libraries

With the introduction of microprocessors for use in library activities, library automation entered into another era in the 1980s:

- — The use of general purpose digital computers for the purpose of automating the house-keeping operations and for the design and development of information retrieval system—early 1960s.
- — Feasibility studies on on-line interactive systems and advanced micro-image searching system—late 1960s.
- — The design of on-line systems and conversion of batch systems to the on-line mode—during 1970s.
- — Exhaustive use of on-line systems and use of mini and microcomputers especially the microprocessors—early 1980s.

Hence, the application of computers in libraries and information centres has brought new dimensions to the users' services. There are several reasons to support the harnessing of computers in libraries. A machine-readable record, prepared at the time of acquisition may be used repetitively for several purposes. Thus a considerable saving in effort, time and resources normally involved in manual processing, can be achieved.

The following are the reasons for the use of computers:

(i) To have control over and improve collection,

(ii) To have better control over the entire operations,

(iii) To improve the existing services and plan for future services,

(iv) To share the resources among various libraries locally and nationally.

The bibliographic data in a library have certain characteristics, which compel the introduction of mechanisation. The characteristics of library data are:

(a) Largely textual in nature.

(b) The library/bibliographic record is of variable length.

(c) Updating of information/files, e.g. deleting and inserting is done almost every day.

The application of computer can be categorised into the following three types:

(i) To support clerical functions associated with technical processing and circulation work.

(ii) For information storage, retrieval and dissemination.

(iii) To support Management Information Services (MIS) for librarians, especially in analysing library statistics.

Besides, the application of computers offers a new dimension of cooperation among libraries. The importance of computers in the creation of library networks has now been realised.

House-keeping Operations

Activities related to acquisition of books, classification, cataloguing, book circulation, serial control, stock verification and book maintenance are traditionally known as house-keeping operations.

In the field of house-keeping routines, the job description amenable to computerisation in each area is outlined as follows:

Acquisition

An automated acquisition system is expected to perform certain managerial functions in addition to certain clerical functions (such as pre-order searching, creating purchase order, etc.). It is also designed to handle regular receipt, non-receipt, out of print documents with wrong billing, unwanted documents with right billing and so on. The following are the typical functions of an automated acquisition control system:

1. Creating purchasing orders (order work).
2. Selection of material.
3. Pre-order searching, especially to avoid duplicate orders.
4. Verification of books with order file and invoices.
5. Updating record file (maintenance of accounts).
6. Accession work.
7. Print out received and not received documents.
8. Claim for damaged materials.
9. Control of book budget (expenditure incurred and balance).

In addition to the above, list of orders and various reports of statistical analyses may also be derived from the system. Provision can also be made in the system to perform such functions as:

(i) To hold orders until funds become available,

(ii) To re-order from a second vendor if the first cannot supply the documents, and

(iii) To compute vendor performance measure.

Cataloguing

During 1960s computers were used in cataloguing but in batch processing system. In batch processing, data were punched in cards and then transformed in the paper tape or magnetic tape. Gradually, programmings were made on the magnetic tape or discs which could be manipulated automatically. But during 1960 to 1970 different libraries started using different types of computers and procedures and there was no uniformity in the catalogue card format.

As a result two aspects of cataloguing system developed and became vital for computerised cataloguing. These are the standardisation of the catalogue entry with the standard bibliographic description having a unique identification mark for each document with the International Standard Book Number (ISBN) and shared cataloguing under a computerised library system using MARC format.

The main activity of cataloguing systems is the production of catalogue cards. In recent years, catalogues in microfiche are becoming very popular since they are least expensive and more durable than book catalogues. In a computer aided cataloguing system, we can also produce, as a by-product of it, spine labels, book pockets and book cards for use in circulation systems. Also it helps us to provide most economically cataloguing information to branch libraries.

MARC (Machine Readable Catalogues)

MARC is an acronym for Machine Readable Catalogue. MARC record is a standard bibliographic description in machine readable form, designed by the Library of Congress (LC), USA.

Among the developments of MARC, the most important development is the programme of the Library of Congress for distribution of catalogue data in tape form. From these tapes, any library in the world can economically acquire machine-readable catalogue data, just as it has been able to acquire catalogue cards. The basic machine-readable catalogue record on a MARC tape consists of the Leader, the Record Directory, the Control Fields and the Variable Fields.

LEADER	RECORD DIRECTORY	CONTROL FIELDS	VARIABLE FIELDS

At present, a growing number of vendors supply the MARC database on CD-ROM disks or digital optical videodiscs accompanied by software which supports the retrieval of specific cataloguing records and the printing of card sets.

Uses of MARC

1. A centrally prepared catalogue can be distributed to the receiving libraries in a machine-readable form.
2. Up-to-date maintenance is possible without employing additional staff.
3. The MARC system is cheaper than the LC catalogue cards.
4. It is useful in providing computerised SDI service.
5. It automatically performs resource-sharing functions.

The following are typical functions of an automated cataloguing system:

1. To prepare thesaurus or subject heading list.
2. Arrangement of catalogue cards into classified, alphabetical or subjectwise order.
3. Preparation of shelf-list.
4. To prepare the list of catalogued items in any desirable form.
5. Cooperative, shared and centralised cataloguing is possible.

Circulation

Circulation control is mainly concerned with the clerical functions of keeping track of documents taken out of the library by the user. In other words, the activities which include charging and discharging, overdue control, reservation and associated file maintenance come under circulation control.

In this section, one can see the flow of reading materials controlled by library operations. It is also the duty of this section to check misuse and promote proper use of library documents. At the same time, it is necessary to record the movement of materials, and to maintain statistics in order to display strength and weakness of stock and provide guidance for collection development in future.

Circulation control is one of the most widely automated library operations, and it is often the first activity that libraries consider automating.

The following are the functions of the computer-based circulation control system:

1. Registration of members.
2. Charging and discharging.
3. Preparing of overdues and recall notices.
4. Updating the record file.
5. Reservation of books and maintenance of inter-library loan.
6. Maintenance of statistics regarding the number of books issued, returned and in other variety of forms.
7. Provision for printing due date slips automatically, generating orders for lost books or additional copies and printing mailing labels for remote borrowers.

User Identification Number (UIN)

To have effective circulation control system, each member of a given library must be assigned an individual number. It is known as User Identification Number (UIN). The UIN is typed for each transaction. It can be any one of the following:

(a) Roll numbers or Registered numbers assigned by the library or parent organization.

(b) Social security or insurance number, if any.

(c) Name.

Serial Control

Computerisation of serials control system helps us to handle processing of serials more easily, quickly and economically. The computerised serials control system comprises several sub-systems. They are:

1. Inventory—Preparation of lists of serials in cards and to make input to the computer, designing and implementation of data files.
2. Ordering and acquisition—Selection, ordering and acquisition of serials newly subscribed.
3. Accessions—Receiving of serials, checking-in, placing claims if not received, renewal of subscription, checking gaps, if any, updating of holding records, placing orders for back volumes, preparation of data files, record maintenance, etc.
4. Cataloguing—Preparation of catalogues of serials and other records designed to meet the needs of users.
5. Circulation—Making available serial issues in separate volumes in the bound form, keeping record of circulation, checking and making arrangements for binding, preparation of lists of titles or lists of articles, etc.

The general objectives of an automated serials control system are to handle serials and to maintain holding lists. In order to achieve these objectives, the system must perform the following functions:

1. To provide input of serial data.
2. Ordering new serials.
3. Generating purchase orders and renewal.
4. Cancellation of presently subscribed serials, if necessary.
5. Sending reminders.

6. Claiming the issue, if necessary (such as request for replacement of a defective copy).
7. Selective follow-up of missing issues.
8. Preparation of various lists like:
   (a) List of journals bought
   (b) Bound (back volumes)
   (c) Number of journals cancelled
   (d) The amount spent, balance, etc.
   (e) Number of journals countrywise and subjectwise.

International Serials Control Systems

Automation in libraries has created immense potentialities in standardisation of data at the international level and has opened up a new vista for transfer of and access to information and documents.

In order to maintain international standards in bibliographic descriptions, IFLA initiated the programme of the International Standard Bibliographic Description (ISBD). As a result, the use of International Standard Book Number (ISBN) came into existence. This helps in identifying books.

For identification, ordering and processing of serial publications, the International Standard Serial Number (ISSN) is being used. The ISSN facilitates computerisation of serials catalogue records by providing machine-readable serials records. It also provides access points to the international network of serials publications. It necessitates and promotes computer-based information service on the strength of holdings of serials in various libraries at the international level.

Computer-based Information Services

The information explosion and complexity of information has posed serious problems in respect of its storage, retrieval and dissemination, as the manual and other conventional methods of handling it have proved to be inadequate and ineffective. Man with his ingenuity has successfully overcome these obstacles to a great extent with the result of advancement made in micrographics, reprography, computer and communication technology. It is true that of all the devices invented by man, the computer is by far the most powerful and effective one.

The application of computer to information services comprises:

1. Generation, collection and processing of information
2. Information retrieval
   (a) Indexing ⎤
   (b) Abstracting ⎦—of documents
3. Selective Information Services (e.g. SDI)
4. Current Awareness Service (CAS)
5. Computerised databases (In-house, national and international)
   (a) MEDLARS
   (b) INSPEC
   (c) COMPENDEX
   (d) ERIC
   (e) BIOSIS
   (f) SCISEARCH

   Some of the available machine readable bibliographic databases are interdisciplinary in nature and can be consulted for general reference sources, e.g.:
   (a) LC MARC
   (b) UK MARC
6. To provide on-line catalogue services
7. Searching and providing print-outs of relevant information, e.g. LISA (Library and Information Science Abstract) in CD-ROM.

Information Technology and Libraries

Technologies which can be used to collect, acquire, process, store, transmit, and disseminate information are usually known as information technologies. In other words, the use or application of various processing, micrographics, video recording and other electronic devices for the storage, retrieval, reproduction and dissemination of information is known as 'Information Technology'. It includes:

- microprocessors, input-output devices
- storage devices
- networking devices
- mainframes
- software

The term information technology is used as a synonym to 'microcomputer' and rapid advances have been made in the field of information technology. As a result, the mainframes, minis and microcomputers are all now being used extensively in libraries and technologies ranging from satellites to optical disks are becoming part of the library automation.

Mechanisation of library house-keeping operations performed predominantly by computers is known as library automation. The computers help us in reducing the time wasted on non-productive work and also helps us in getting access to up-to-date information and to share the limited resources effectively. The computers make library service as 'Libraries without Walls', with an ability of free access to world information. At the same time, it does not diminish the role of librarian in this changed scenario, it is being modified to make him an information scientist.

Evolution of Information Technology 11

We are living in an age of 'Information explosion'. Moreover, it is expected from the library managers that the required information must be gushed out immediately and in accuracy. The 'information technology' comprising computers with telecommunication technology, satellite technology, reprographic technology, printing technology and CD-ROM technology comes to the rescue of the librarian in satisfying the needs of the present users. With the onslaught of microcomputers, the library managers could solve the traditional methods of handling information such as storage, processing, retrieval and dissemination mechanically.

Definition

The term Information Technology refers to the Electronic technologies for collecting, storing, processing and communicating information. There are two main categories, which process information, such as computer systems and those, which disseminate information, such as telecommunication systems. The term generally is understood to describe systems that combine both.

According to ALA glossary, "Information Technology is the application of computers and other telecommunication technologies to the acquisition, organization, storage, retrieval and dissemination of information."

With the introduction of new IT, libraries are now expected to make use those technologies to provide nascent information quickly and in greater volume which is globally available than before. In this context, it would be apt to refer to the fourth law of library science, 'To save the time of reader/staff.' On account of exponential growth of information and its sources, the print media is becoming obsolete and the storage media is fast changing in a dramatic manner. The following are some of the novel methods of storage media available:

(a) Print media (papers, metal sheets, etc.)
(b) Film media (microfilm, micro-fiche, etc.)
(c) Magnetic media (magnetic tapes, drums, etc.)
(d) Electronic media (floppy and hard discs, microchips, etc.)
(e) Optical media (CD-ROM, video disc, CD-WORM, CD-I, etc.)

Emergence of Information Society

In the age of Science, the computers can make the libraries and society paperless in future. The world famous futurist, Alvin Toffler predicts the 21st century as 'Space age' and 'Computer age' and even calls it as 'Information age' and 'Electronic era'. Blaise Cronin calls the future society as 'Information society' and predicts the emergence of information workers. The developing countries have reached a stage where the communication technology threatens the very existence of traditional libraries, and it is true with the fact that libraries are being digitalized and traditional libraries are slowly waning and gives place to emergence of a new type of library known as digital library in other words 'Virtual Library'.

A developing country like India with sparse resources needs to educate millions of its library users in conceptualizing their information needs and matching them with the resources of the library by comprehending the methodology of the library. It is generally felt that any invention which does not reach the last man, the same would die a natural death, but in the case of IT the impact of computer and telecommunication technologies have already become one with the people.

The problem we face today is not the dearth of information, rather it is excessive information. Almost in all the fields abstracts are available, but even these have become so numerous that abstracts of various abstracting services are necessary. With deluge of information the traditional library with its system cannot process, store and distribute to the users. Hence, there is a need for introduction of microcomputers which have revolutionized the management of information in relation to speed, accuracy. Efficiency and effectiveness, which was not possible otherwise. The microcomputers with telecommunication technologies have enabled the users to have instant access to digitized information and provided services like paper to paperless forms including multimedia.

India and IT

With the advent of information technology, information programmers like NISSAT, NILNET, INDONET, INSDOC and SENDOC are being evolved and generated successfully in India. There are about 20 organizations in India, which offer, computerized bibliographical information services. Among them, INDONET has an integrated information management and distributed data processing facility spanning the entire country. A new attempt has been made to get databases from various national and international organizations and make them accessible on-line through INDONET. And also an international gateway in Mumbai is set up the cooperation of Videsh Sanchar Nigam Limited (VSNL) to enable Indian users to access international databases available form LOCKHEED/DIALOG, SDC/ORBIT, ESANET, etc.

All is well with the special libraries in India, where a maximum harnessing of information is taking place with the help of IT. In the case of academic libraries, the condition is reversed. Though the UGC, the apex body of Universities and colleges in India in relation to finance, only a few universities are automated and the rest of them are only in infant stage, INFLIBNET, a part of UGC financially assisting both universities and college libraries to automate their library operations. In spite of such efforts, there seems to be very little efforts in the direction of introducing the technological developments in the academic and public libraries in India, this may be due to:

1. Non-availability of skilled personnel.
2. Lack of training opportunities to handle sophisticated tools and machineries.
3. Lack of motivation and awareness on the part of the library managers.
4. Financial crunch.

Digital Libraries

The digital library concept has emerged very recently and being deeply rooted in the field of library and information science. Organizations where information is being handled are increasingly replacing conventional storage, process and retrieval systems with digital systems. On account of discrete analysis of documents, the conversion from manual to digital is inevitable. Hence, the digital medium is fast replacing paper in a dramatic revolution.

Digital libraries aim to provide ready access to the storehouse of information. Generally, the digital libraries specialize in storing a particular subject field of information, which will be interwoven together with the other participating libraries. Digital libraries combine communication technology and information source and allow remote access of its resources to other libraries by breaking down the physical barriers through national and international computer networks. The suitable example of this is INTERNET.

In the context of information explosion, large amount of information is being generated every moment. This resulted in harnessing the use of information technology in the field of library and information services to serve the diversified users. With the electronic devices, the information can be rearranged, selected marshaled and transformed enormous data at phenomenal speed. Hence, the libraries and information Centers are expected to use various types of technologies to provide information more quickly and in greater volume than before.

The use of electronics has a great relevance in the contest of fourth law of library science "Save the time of the Reader." In this context, Dr. S.R. Ranganathan laid emphasis on the internal efficiency of the library. The Information Technology provides better needs of transmission of data or text in the form of written or printed records. Zorkolzy has analyzed information technology from four different viewpoints such as society economics, technology and the individual and also mentions the following four features that affect the quality of information, such as:

(a) Accuracy
(b) Content (the breadth/scope)
(c) Regency
(d) Frequency of presentation.

Objectives of Information Technology

The information technology and communication technology have revolutionized the activities of library and information system. They enable the users to access enormous information at the tremendous speed. The overall impact of information technology on library and information science, can be viewed with the following three major divisions:

1. Impact on the technical services
2. Impact of public services
3. Impact on library organization structure.

The following objectives can be deduced into the following groups:

(a) Supporting technical functions associated with technical processing and Circulation work.
(b) Supporting information storage, retrieval and dissemination systems.
(c) Supporting, management information services for libraries, especially Analyzing library statistics.
(d) It can best be used in service and orientation courses for practicing librarians, continuing education programmes for teachers of library and information

science, correspondence studies and library extension services.

(e) It paves the way for networking of libraries to promote research and consortium of national libraries.

Information Age

The impact of information technology is described by different futurists in many different words. Some called it as "Information Age", "Information Society", "Paperless Society", "Global Village", "Electronic Libraries", "Digital Libraries" and so on.

The coordination direction and control of all social activity depend on information. The age of information that we have entered is in many ways analogous to the age of energy that stridulated the industrial revolution.

Dr. Coates identified the following as the striking developments in information technology, which are in vogue:

- Digitization of all data
- New and more natural user interfaces
- Increasing mobility of information technology
- Specialization, miniaturization and dispersion of information technology
- Multipurpose technology of broader capability and greater flexibility
- The networking of networks and so on.

Information Superhighway

The vision of 'Information Superhighway' is nothing but an unprecedented nationalized and eventually worldwide electronics communications network that connects every one to every one else and provides just about any sort of electronic communication imaginable. The purpose is to provide accessibility for remote banking, schooling, shopping, taxpaying, chatting, game playing, videoconferencing, medical diagnosing and so on. In other words, the information highway is an embellishment of Internet as existing global tapestry of computer networks.

The author William Gibson popularized another popular term "cyberspace". The term cyberspace exists only as digital bits stored or travelling in a computer network. The closest thing we have true cyberspace today is Internet.

Marketing of Information

Ever since the invention of satellite communication, the information has been undergoing sea change. The development and consequence of information revolution is co-related to growth on information technologies. This resulted in increasing in speed and volume of transmitting information. New technologies and techniques bring changes in the information management. Contemporary, conventional and modern management systems recognize that marketing is an essential component of any organization or institution's work plan. Even the products and services of organizations are noteworthy and if the consumers of users do not know them, the products would not reach the target groups. Libraries being the institutions, which transfer the knowledge and content to the society need to make available the resources they keep to the users. The current society is the knowledge-driven one; the knowledge of technology makes the society and country stronger.

Information as a Commodity

The world is moving towards a knowledge-based society for which information is of primary importance. The last decade national and international initiatives have emerged to establish information infrastructures, aimed at increasing the use of information to a wide variety of users. Hence, in implementing information systems, much focus is given to view information as a commodity like any other product.

Knowledge production needs investment of time, energy, cost, etc. Information and decision-making clearly has a cost, time personnel, money and other related factors. The cost of creating knowledge structure even is not measured in direct terms, people used to find the means of some forms of measuring the cost of it. The information produced as a result of human efforts is available as a commodity and naturally against the payment. The fact of understanding the time spent for making lists, thinking, organizing and other related activities leads to conclude that information produced is available against money.

The cost of making a decision, weighing all factors to do and arriving at an ultimate decision can be high and time-consuming. The indirect way in many situations to fix the cost of information product is by accounting the time one has invested. This happens in the production of software. In many cases, the price of software by taking primarily the idea, plan and innovativeness of the products besides the total time taken for producing the product.

The following factors would augment the view that information is commodity:

1. **Information Economy**. It is true that we get information for cost, able to sell it for cost, as information is a product. Information is less influenced by incremental costs and it is liable to have an infinite distribution of a single ideal since intellectual property rights hold well for information production, it is measurable as product.
2. **Industrial Economy**. In industrial economy, the technological increase is more. In achieving economy of production, people consider commodities base, short-term goods and long-term goods, incremental costs of production and the property rights issues increase and in such situation information needs are high.
3. **Service Economy**. In service economy, labour base, labour management and other related activities need proper services drawn from different factors. The service economy is technology based. The incremental costs are significant in the service economy and ultimately the information is needed for effective service. Thus, information has all the characteristics of a commodity and now being treated and sold like a product.

Concept of Marketing

Philip Kotler described marketing as "the art of helping your customer become better off". The modern concept also emphasizes that marketing is customer-oriented and the customer centred concept lay down emphasis on the users' involvement to a greater degree. The term marketing is also described as the process of planning and executing the conception, pricing and promotion and distribution of ideas, goods and services to create exchanges that satisfy individual and organizational objectives. Thus, the marketing is not confined only to products, but extended to services, ideas, knowledge and information.

Those working in the information industry can be categorized into two, those 'not-for-profit', and 'for-profit'. Those not-for-profit organizations also cannot make a loss in the sense; they must remain within their budget. They too should market the information for their very survival or for a justifiable expansion programme. Thus, marketing of information is becoming an important subject.

There are a number of factors, which bear up on the emerging information industry, which might be considered under such headings as:

1. Market characteristics;
2. Services offered;
3. Competition;
4. Government activity; and
5. Technology.

Whether marketing is essential for libraries and information centers? Since libraries function mainly as not-for-profit organizations, the marketing concept is not required. This feeling tends to occupy the mind of many library and information professionals. The following are the factors that necessitate the marketing of information products and services:

1. Each institution wishes to achieve high levels of customer satisfaction.
2. Each wants to enhance the perceived value of their services.
3. Both want to insure the survival of their respective institutions.

Impact of Information Technology on Library Services

The impact of new technologies is seen in all walks of life. It has changed and enhanced the routine of library work in relation to collection, storage and transmission of information with great speed. The basic concept in the use of new technology is to free the information scientists from the routine jobs connected with library operations, which can be entrusted to computer.

The electronic computers provide information, which helps to reduce the bulk of the printed materials. The computers also help to make the libraries and society paperless in near future. The developing counties like India have reached a stage where the communication technology threatens the very existence of traditional libraries.

The emerging communication technologies, especially the interactive digital devices will drive the information. The technology can handle the data overload out a human being cannot. It is the use of information technology that will give librarians as audience, an attitude, an amplification of self that will raise their status in life.

The convergence of computer, telecommunication and IT electronics formed the basis for an advance information society. The following are the main influence of information technology, which has a direct impact on information society, they are:

Increased computer power leading to faster and cheaper computer processing paved way for automation of all libraries even with low budget with the latest telecommunication technologies like ISDN (Integrated Service Digital Network) the data transmission capacity can be increased which facilitated with introduction of a varied new services such as E-collection, E-journals, E-mail teleconferencing, E-clippings and E-publishing and networks. The optical storage media, which is the cheapest data storage device, has increased the storage capacity of the libraries.

Digitization of information such as texts, graphics, audio, video that provide quick transmission of any type of data with great speed.

The high capacity and reliable hardware, server, software and client node have increased the performance efficiency.

The utility software, which functions as user friendly has enhanced the interface between technology and users of the library.

Library as Communication Agency

Advances in library automation also made possible the rapid development of union lists of serials, arranging holding information for a number of libraries. Library networks made available central agency that could assemble, merge and maintain the bibliographic and holding information of other libraries. The development of technology has provided significant improvement in "resource sharing", especially in inter-library loan operations.

The recent advancement in communication technology has created more awareness about information use and it has resulted in increasing library services. The future libraries may not be recognized by their size but by the variety of services and approaches, where information search areas will be outlined.

The objective of any library is to communicate the contents of the printed and non-printed materials to those whom such contents are of immense use. The information center is the bridge between the stored information and the individual who needs such information. The day has dawned that the libraries are required to Marshall different combinations of communication technology for the benefit and progress of a nation.

Application of Internet in Libraries

Internet is truncated version of internetworking, which refers to interconnecting two or more computer networks. A computer network is interconnection of autonomous computing systems through communication systems through a communication media. The major goals of networking are to felicitate resource sharing and communication among users connected to hosts. Internet, being network of networks, has the same major goals and spans across the entire globe, compares to limited geophysical are covered by local area and wide area networks. Thus the Internet can be thought of as vast pool of computers, people and information spread across the entire world.

Internet is an immensely popular worldwide network of on-line users. Almost anything can be a subject of discussion on the Internet, which area formed for their chat shows. Those with intellectual property banks, libraries, research agencies. Government archives use the Internet to bring people closer. The

Internet is very useful to the librarian in discharging various functions such as:

– Acquisitions
– Cataloguing
– Documentation
– Collection development.

The Internet has brought about a new academic culture of understanding and cooperation. It is the gateway for libraries and information centers to enter the electronic information era. Its combination with contemporary technology has transformed digital information which used to be mostly textual in nature, into multimedia information, thereby they have knowledge about things instead of just information about them. Electronic publication has become complements to hard print copies. They are inexpensive, easily accessible and ecologically congenial.

The Internet can provide access to essentially unlimited sources of information not conveniently obtainable through other means. Libraries have recognized the importance of information providing rather than the collection development. The Internet has made possible the concept of a virtual library, which is an information service or a resource, which can be accessed via a telecommunication network. It enables information professionals to take advantages of such unimaginable potential. Further, the users who are at campus or off campus can use the Internet at all hours, across distances. Student study groups can work together on-line, faculty members can held electronic office hours in addition to their regular office hours. Therefore, the Internet works to create a significant new form, a limitless number of electronic rooms and space where one of the most fundamental educational process—energetic discussion and debate can be carried on continuously.

The information scientist can render almost all services through Internet similar to those provided in traditional libraries. In Internet environment, the services of library are available through library home page or its parent body home page. The prerequisite for opening/maintaining Internet is the usage of information technology and the knowledge of Internet application such as web browsers, preparing documents in HTML format, etc.

In the modern information technology age, the librarianship is facing great challenges. In the networked environment if the end user can directly access the desired information, what role do the librarian and the information center have to play? Will the libraries end up as 'archives' for maintaining old print publications? Several exciting possibilities exist, but first librarian has to make a transition to network librarian and information professional to network information professional.

The following are the strategies to meet the challenges posed by the information technology:

- To device strategies to meet the challenges in the light of the five laws of library science.
- To change mind-set and enter electronics era by revising professional methods, techniques and tools.
- To re-modal professional education and training to meet new demands and challenges.
- To study, understand, explore, expand and apply Dr. Ranganathan's seminal ideas for professional development and meeting new challenges.
- To promote research and development to contribute to solving problems of information technology and networking and information services to meet user needs in a digital era.
- Of all information delivery systems that exist in our society, none is so pivotal as the library. Libraries can deliver information across time and space but they fail to serve, if they do not focus on delivery.
- Libraries in the future survive because of strategic expertise and leadership skills, not so much on technological knowledge or financial resources.

Digital Library

12

Introduction

A digital library is not merely a collection of electronic information. It is an organized and digitized system of data that can serve as a rich resource for its user community. 'Digital Libraries' are also called as 'Electronic Libraries'. The latest techniques in information technology for effective knowledge organization are the expert system and hypertext which are the effective tools for information. As a concept, digital library has different connotations for different professional groups. To the information science community, it represents a new means of extending and enhancing access to distribute in other words remote information resources. The digital libraries widen the access to broader level of users and provide new opportunities for the library and information professionals to enhance theoretical background and practical approach. It has been a persistent endeavour of our society to develop newer means and mechanism for expressing, recording, archiving and dissemination ideas and knowledge. In the concept of digital libraries the "Digital Asset Management" is the new method of creating a permanent repository of human knowledge, which is accessible globally.

The digital libraries facilitate the global access to the universe of knowledge. The roots of present day digital libraries may be traced back to the advent of the hypertext systems. Digital libraries have evolved based on the techniques and principles developed by Vennevar Bush who designed a system called

"Memex". The concept of digital library is a global phenomenon and the libraries have started connecting other libraries in distance places by wide area network. In India networks such as, INFLIBNET, DELNET, CALIBNET, etc., are successfully working to share the resources of different libraries.

The revolutions in the past namely:

(a) Agricultural revolution,
(b) Industrial revolution, and
(c) Technological revolution.

Brought sea change in our physical, social economic and political environment. Currently the world is experiencing yet another revolution known as Information Revolution. This has effected with the onslaught of computer and repro- and micrographic technologies.

The futurologist Alvin Toffler in his *Future Shock* mentions technologies are leading us to the third wave; the first two being the agriculture and industrial wave. Hence, it is necessary that the library and information professionals must possess knowledge of global information resources, information services, systems of generating, managing the information skills.

Digitization

The process of converting analogue information to a digital format is known digitization. In communication technology this is the process of converting analogue signals to digital signals. In information system digitization often refers to the process of converting an image some type of scanning device into digital representation so that it can be displayed on a screen and manipulated.

Definition of Digital Library

The term digital libraries may be defined as the new week of carrying out the functions of libraries encompassing new types of information resources new approaches to acquisition, new methods of storage preservation and dissemination and new approaches to cataloguing and classification.

In nutshell the digital libraries are defined as libraries, which have number of machine-readable publications and facilities for remote access to several databases. In other words it is a distributed text-based computerized information system and may have several provisions to access documents, mostly from outside the organization.

The standard Digital Library project states that the "Integrated digital library will create a shared environment linking everything—personal information collection to collection of conventional libraries to large data collection shared scientist. Integrated virtual libraries provide on array of new services, uniform access to networked information."

According to Williams Saffady, the digital library may be:

1. Machine-readable data files, often with scientific and technical applications.
2. Components of the emerging National information infrastructure.
3. Various on-line databases and CD-ROM information products.
4. Computer storage devices on which information resides, such as optical disk.
5. Computerized networked library systems.

Based on the above concepts he gave the following definition for a digital library: "Digital library is a library that maintains all, or substantial part, of its collection in computer-processible form as an alternative, supplement, or complement to the conventional printed and microfilm materials that currently dominate library collections."

In other words, we can safely say that a digital library is one in which the controlled collections are in digital form, and the access to this digital information is based upon digital technology. Thus a digital library is different from a traditional library. The digital library may be defined as the new way of carrying out. The functions of libraries encompassing new types of information resources, new approaches to acquisition, new methods of storage and preservation, new approaches to classification and cataloguing, intensive use of electronic systems and networks and dramatic shifts in intellectual, organizational and electronic practices. It is also known as a distributed text-based computerized information system and services. It may have several provisions to access documents, those areas of high value, mostly from libraries to libraries, which have number of machine-readable publications and facilities for remote access to several databases.

Foundations of Digital Library

As a result of information explosion, the distribution of information started playing a key role for humankind for development. Limitation in access to such information leads to look for some innovative method known as information technology. This resulted in introduction of structured information or data using international standard ISO 8879 in other words "SGML". This helped as in presenting features and distribution of information on both paper as well as electronic medium without duplicating efforts. The information presented in the structured format is defined as database. The database can be divided into four types.

They are:

(1) Full test database (Books and journals).

(2) Bibliographic and directory database.

(3) Multimedia database (audio video).

(4) Image database.

The Digital library consists of digital information storage/retrieval servers and client nodes that are connected to each other through retrieval servers and client nodes that are connected to each other through INTERNET and INTRANET. The retrieval of information from client nodes should be made easy with Graphical User Interface (GUI) and Web Based Access (WBA). The retrieval of information through Digital library requires the following for better result:

(a) High end servers.

(b) Scanner and multimedia infrastructure.

The above-mentioned infrastructure is required to digitize, archive and retrieve library e-documents.

Digital libraries store materials in electronic format and manipulate large collections of those materials effectively. Hence, research into digital libraries is really research into network information systems. The key technological issues are how to search and display desired selections from and across large collections. Which practical digital libraries must focus on issues of access? Costs and digitization technology, digital library research concentrates on how to develop the necessary infrastructure for effective mass manipulation of the information on the networks.

Knowledge and information in the digital environments reveal a fast growth. In the libraries today most of it is available in the form of printed documents, while on the Internet and through the digital documents it is available in the digital form. In the printed form the ideas are almost sealed on the pages, while in the digital form they can be accessed simultaneously by any number of users. This makes the role of the libraries that have only printed documents with them very limited in scope in the present day world.

Over these years, the world of information has undergone a sea change and a good deal of transformation has taken place in collecting, storing, disseminating and publishing of information. Peter Young brings out the changes that have taken over the past three decades that characterize a transition from a modern era to a post-modern age. The changes that have become possible due to the computer and telecommunication technologies are leaving a major impact on the libraries.

From Modern Era	To Post-modern Age
Fixed, permanent, formatted text	fluid and transient multimedia
Collections	resources
Static library facilities with information	free, flexible and virtual
Fixed stacks	spaces
Uniform sources, citations, annotation/transient	and customized

(Contd....)

From Modern Era	To Post-modern Age
References	works
Services provided to individual readers collaborative teams	tailored services to
Standard reference services analysis	personalized consulting and
Professionally provided	integrated service provision services
Locally owned permanent collections system	holistic, integrated networked
Centralized collections and services global access	distributed, decentralized
Hierarchical organizational structures relationships	participative and collegial
Discipline specialization studies	inter-multi, cross-disciplinary
Generic user service offerings services	user-/use-specific relevant
Formal publication acquisition formal	integration of informal with

Digital Asset Management

Information explosion has resulted in rapid proliferation in the number of digital files stored and the range of people requiring accessing them. Without proper innovative method of organization, the simple tasks such as locating an existing image, graphic or logo can be time consuming and costly. Hence, the focus is on the management of organizations with electronic files. These are documents created, communicated, received and used in electronic form and those converted from paper to electronic form.

Digital asset management is a business process and a decision-making framework that extended time horizon, draws from economics as well as engineering and considers a broad range of assets. Asset management has come of age because of:

(a) Changes in the environment,

(b) Changes in public expectations, and

(c) Extraordinary advances in technology.

Impact of Multimedia on Library Services

Multimedia is a combination of some or all forms such as text, data images, photographs, animation, audio and video, which are converted from different formats into a uniformat digital media and is delivered by computers. Unlike the analogue media, the digital media which allows users to manipulate according to the needs. Use at their pace, and interact at any point of the program when a multimedia program is developed in a hypertext environment, the resulting product is called 'hypermedia'; hence multimedia would then be a part of the hypermedia products but not *vice versa*. The basic difference between these two is in the organization and linkage of the information fragments. The information fragments in multimedia are organized linearly whereas in hypermedia, these are non-linearly organized with links to each other.

The main elements of the multimedia are:

TEXT :	Information about an object or event, etc. notes, captions, subtitles, contents, indexes, dictionaries and help facilities.
DATA :	Tables, charts, graphs, spreadsheets, statistics and raw data.
GRAPHICS :	Both traditional and computer generated such as drawings, Points, maps, etc.
PHOTOGRAPHIC IMAGES :	Negatives, slides, prints, video cameras.
ANIMATION :	Including both computer generated, video, etc.
AUDIO :	It includes speech and music digitized form cassettes, tapes, CDs, etc.

The impact of multimedia on library services not only helps the users in providing information from different media on one platform, but also saves on space, money, maintenance, operational inconveniences, etc. The major advantages of multimedia in libraries are:

1. It can help satisfying different information needs such as reference, enrichment, entertainment, leisure, etc.
2. It can help meeting various types of information preference of the users such as scholarly, scientific, vocational, artistic, recreational, etc.
3. Being a digital format, information can also be accessed by remote users on a network and also helps in overcoming the accommodate users.
4. It is interesting and easy to use over the existing form such as print microforms, online, etc.
5. Its control and interactivity helps the users and provides the benefits of books and human beings.

Hybrid Library

A hybrid library is not just a traditional library (which contains paper-based resources) or just a virtual library (which contains electronic resources), but somewhere between the two. It is a library, which brings together a range of different information sources, printed and electronic, local and remote, in a seamless way. Hence the hybrid library is envisaged as the bringing together of technologies from new developments from electronic, digital or virtual library which have been taking place around the world. In the rapidly changing information environment, academic information is increasingly being published in electronic format, although the vast majority of information sources that appear in electronic format remained linked to paper-based information carriers. In the hybrid library, the needs of the information user are satisfied in that the library's information system refers him/her directly and seamlessly to appropriate sources, which are made available either from the library's collection or through inter-lending or directly from an electronic service.

The hybrid library was designed to bring a range of technologies from different sources together in the context of a working library and to begin to explore integrated systems and services in both the electronic and print environments. The following are the features of hybrid libraries:

1. User authentication,
2. Registration and induction,
3. Ordering and delivery of materials,
4. Metadata indexing for printed and electronic information resources,
5. Teaching and learning support packages,
6. Extended possibilities for on-line publication and digitization,
7. User-managed resource discovery techniques, and
8. Access gateways using all protocols.

The concept of hybrid library encapsulates the notion that major institutions will have to work in an environment where access will have to be provided to a wider than ever range of material types. Further, there is an ambition to ensure for integrated access to this range of resources. The pragmatic view of the future of libraries would suggest that it is likely that most libraries will for the foreseeable future—which after all is not all that long—base their services on a mix of physical objects (books, paper-based journals, videotapes and the like) and electronic stuff (web pages, remote data services, CD-ROMs, etc.). For this reason, approaches that stress the management and delivery of 'hybrid library' services would appear to be the most useful. Crawford (1999), who argues somewhat controversially that 'the glory days of the all-digital brigade seem to be in the past', refers to 'ever-shifting complex combinations of digital and analog collections' which, as noted above, he terms 'complex libraries'.

The most widely used definition of the hybrid library is that provided by Rusbridge (1998): "The hybrid library was designed to bring a range of technologies from different sources together in the context of working library, and also to begin to explore integrated systems and services in both the electronic and print environments. The hybrid library should integrate access to all kinds of resources using different technologies from the digital library world, and across different media." Now the challenge for library managers is to create integrated services, which provide a 'seamless' service to the user. The user should be able to access services through consistent interfaces, which provide compatible features. The hybrid library should not, however, be homogeneous and it should be able to adjust its services to the needs and rights of each user—for example, by 'remembering' previous search strategies, by storing details of the user groups to which the individual belongs and by 'knowing' the user's willingness to pay for premium services.

Intellectual Property Right

Products of the human intellect considered as personal property, especially works protected under the copyright and inventions protected by patents. Other subjects include utility models, industrial designs, confidential information and trade marks. The concept of intellectual property may be divided into physical, tangible things and intangible, incorporeal property. Intellectual property falls into the latter category. When a property right in a written work first came to be recognized, ownership by the printer-publisher was important, not that of the author. Patents originated as monopolies granted by royal letters patent not only for inventions but also for other valuable items of commerce. Hence, the two most important forms of intellectual property are COPYRIGHT and PATENTS.

Copyright

A legal concept, which concerns rights to copy. Copyright protects the labour, skill and judgment which someone—author, artist or some other creator—expends in the creation of an original piece of work, whether it is a so-called 'literary work', a piece of music, a painting, a photograph, TV programme or any other created work. Copyright is a major issue in digital libraries. Here copyright means licences and the licences are required for all access, whether implied or explicit. It is the legal protection extended to the owner of the creator in an original work that he has created. It comprises two main sets of rights, i.e. the economic rights and the moral rights. It means the protection is only extended to the form in which an idea is expressed, but not to the concepts, methods and ideas that are expressed. Copyright protection is provided to the authors of original works of authorship, including literary, artistic and scientific works. The owners of copyright can generally prevent the unauthorized reproduction, distribution, sale and adaptation of an original work. The protection generally lasts for the life of the author plus fifty years or more in the case of works belonging to corporate bodies. Works covered under copyrights are:

1. Literary works.
2. Musical and artistic works including any accompanying works.
3. Dramatic works including any accompanying material.
4. Pantomimes and choreographic works.
5. Pictorial graphic sculptural works.
6. Motion pictures and other audio-visual works.
7. Sound records.
8. Architectural works.

In no case does copyright protection for an original work of authorship extend to any idea, procedure, process, system, method of operation, concept, principle or discovery, regardless of the form in which it is described, explained, illustrated or embodied in such work.

Indian Scenario of Copyright

The Copyright (Amendment) Act, 1994, which came into force from May 1995, enlarged the scope of the term 'author' to mean 'in relation to any literary, dramatic, musical or artistic work which is computer generated the person who causes the work to be created'. The enlargement of the meaning of the term author also means the creators of the computer generated literary, artistic, dramatic and musical works covered under the ambit of copyright. The definition of "literary work" was amended to include the computer programmes, tables and compilations including computer databases. A computer programme is defined as a set of instructions expressed in words codes, schemes or in any other form including a machine-readable medium, capable of causing a computer to perform a particular task or achieve a particular result.

The Act 1957 allows making of copies of computer software by the lawful buyer for fair use. It is not infringement if the copies are made to utilize the computer software for the purpose for which it was supplied or to make back up copies purely as a temporary protection against loss, destruction or damage. As per the Section 52 of the Act, if a person knowingly makes use of a copy of a computer programme for (personal) gain in the course of trade or business, it is treated as an infringement of copyright. The amended Act also protects the creators of the computer-generated works and includes computer programmes, tables and compilations including computer databases.

In the face of technological developments, the present copyright laws are not able to prevent piracy infringement of rights. Small-scale violations, which do not conflict with owners' rights, may have to be accepted as a part of fair use for at least some more time. Also, the current copyright laws have to be heavily modified to suit to the digital and networked environment. It is envisaged that the electronic file transfer would replace inter-library loan and photo-duplication in near future. This can lead to many issues as in a networked environment. A digital document can potentially replace all printed copies and still can be accessed by multiple users simultaneously. Remote access and downloading can virtually make one single document enough for all the libraries and users of the network.

Conclusion

In the age of information, easy access to information is an essential prerequisite for the development of a country and access to information is also a hallmark of democracy. Hence, the developing countries like India should make earnest efforts to concentrate more on developing and using new electronic gadgets that provide better access to information. There are very many approaches to modeling the digital library, but a number of common features emerge from the research and development that has taken place in recent years. These are:

1. Recognition that in the real world the information of interests to digital library users is to be found in a range of heterogeneous databases and collections, physically distributed but connected by electronic networks and containing objects of many different types.
2. Distributed ownership and rights, including complex intellectual property rights.
3. A need to provide organization, provenance and authority for items and collections.
4. A wide range of users with a variety of client systems operation within a broad selection of environments and pursuing many different purposes.
5. A business needs to control access to resources although the models, and especially the economic models, are far from clear.
6. A role, variously defined, for a broker or other intermediary, which connects the users to the resources of interest to them.
7. A range of standards and protocols, for describing resources, for encoding them and for delivering them, including for searching and retrieval; many existing systems cannot inter-operate effectively and there is thus a pressing need to agree open standards.

E-Collection and Resources

13

Electronic Library

The term "Electronic Library" is generally described as an organized and managed collection of information in a variety of formats such as structured data text, image audio, video and graphics all in digital form. The collection in Electronic library is organized and managed for the benefit of users in easy access to its contents. This includes a number of search or navigation aids that would operate within that particular library and allow access to other collections of information connected by networks worldwide (INTERNET).

The term electronic library is not a new concept. As early as 1940s, President Roosevelt's scientific adviser Vannevar Bush was dreaming of a model for a hypertext-linked virtual library. The Xanadu project, a worldwide hypertext-link publishing system with automatic royalty control, was a later development in the same direction. With advances in information technology and, in particular, the inception, and phenomenal growth of the World Wide Web, the electronic library or e-library is today very much within grasp. A library that holds a collection of resources in electronic format has the technology in terms of a database management system, a LAN, and access to Internet, and skilled and motivated personnel has the potential of developing an e-library with minimal investment in time or money.

E-Collection

The term e-collection refers to digitized documents that are archived and available for retrieval to users without wasting his/

her time in getting the right information at the right time. The e-collection in the library is imperative on the following reasons:

(a) The ever-escalating price rise of books and increase in subscription rates.

(b) The copyright has become a central issue among libraries, educators and other users of knowledge resources on the one hand and the producers of documents on the other.

(c) Librarians feel open and free access of all information to Users and Producers (Publishers) want limited free access.

(d) The advancement in telecommunication, Internet technology and the networking technologies have given the library and information centers an opportunity to improve the information services to the patrons in more effective way.

The following are the e-collections that are available in all digital libraries to provide effective service to the users:

(a) E-Books
(b) E-Journals
(c) E-Clippings
(d) E-Content pages
(e) E-Reports
(f) E-Databases

Infrastructure for E-Collection

To build and hosting of e-collections in a library, we require the following infrastructure harnessing the e-resources effectively:

(a) LAN
(b) Scanners
(c) Multimedia infrastructure for content creation
(d) Server class systems for archiving e-documents
(e) Web technologies for publishing e-collections
(f) Desktop access over the internet and intranet
(g) Utility software packages for supporting e-documents.

Designing and establishing the infrastructure in a library is more important since it has got the direct impact on its information services. Hence, LAN with high-speed multi-process servers and powerful workstations for speedy access to information are required to establish pool-proof e-resources. It is clear with the following diagram:

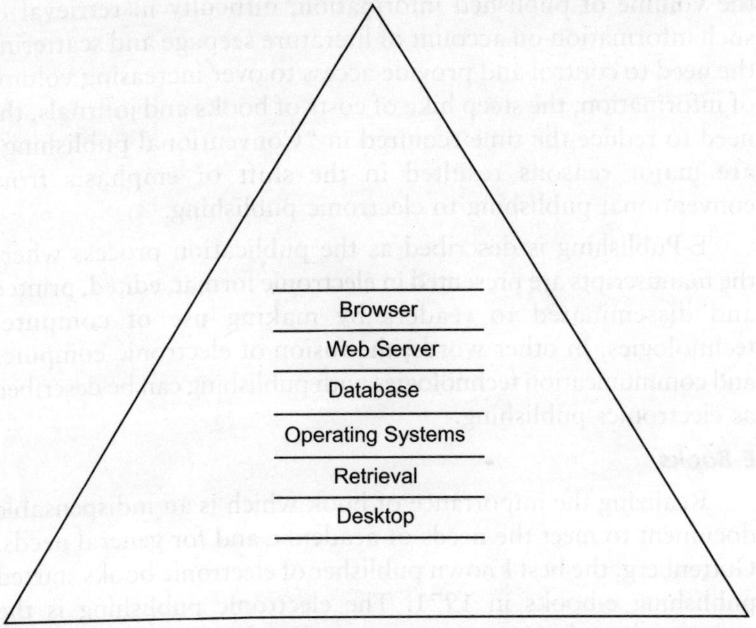

E-Publishing

Technological revolution and information explosion has changed our outlook towards functioning and services of libraries and Information Centers. The library environment is rapidly changing to electronic environment and electronic media like floppy disks, magnetic tapes, CD-ROMs and DVDs, is slowly replacing the physical hard volumes of books and journals. The concept and mode of presentation is changing from static text based to graphic, hypertext, audio, video and now has reached interactive multi-media. To cope with the accelerated growth of journals, steep rise in their prices, decreasing buying powers of the libraries and hike in postal charges particularly for overseas delivery, has led the libraries, publishers and users to opt for e-publishing and e-delivery of documents. The delays in communicating the research results and slowness in the process of traditional form of publishing have led to the popularity of e-publishing.

The information explosion and the exponential growth in the volume of published information, difficulty in retrieval of such information on account of literature seepage and scattering the need to control and provide access to over increasing volume of information, the steep hike of costs of books and journals, the need to reduce the time required in "Conventional publishing" are major reasons resulted in the shift of emphasis from conventional publishing to electronic publishing.

E-Publishing is described as the publication process where the manuscripts are presented in electronic format, edited, printed and disseminated to readers by making use of computer technologies. In other words, the fusion of electronic computer and communication technologies with publishing can be described as electronics publishing.

E-Books

Realizing the importance of book which is an indispensable document to meet the needs of academic and for general needs, Guttenberg, the best known publisher of electronic books started publishing e-books in 1971. The electronic publishing is the process of production of typeset quality documents containing text graphics, images, tables, equations, etc. with the help of a data processing system. In other words e-publishing is the computer aided of assisted publishing. The published information on electronic medium is distributed on state-of-the-art medium through CD-ROM and on-line networks (INTERNET, ISDN, etc.).

The electronic publishing can be represented as:

EP = electronic technology + computer technology + publishing.

In order to achieve quick publishing and dissemination, the publication of a book electronically is encouraged and well received among the academicians and researchers. Realizing the above fact, a number of encyclopedias are available on CD-ROM. By and large, the Internet is not a satisfactory platform for publishing full text of documents but at the same time CD-ROM is a suitable medium for publishing books.

E-books are being produced globally and are becoming available on the Web. Many universities have begun to produce them and for example, the On-Line Books Page of the University of Pennsylvania gives access to more than 12,000 listings. The e-books section of Amazon.com gives access to them on a wide variety of subjects including Biographies, Business, and Children's books, History, Literature including fiction, science and sports. Through this novel publishing, the authors have begun to get substantial royalties on titles that are popular. The issues that hinder the growth of e-books are that content formats and reading devices of e-book reader companies are not inter-operable and electronic transfer calls for a new way to protect copyright. At this stage if we wish to read a particular e-book on our reader, the compatibility issues have to be checked in order to see that the e-book publisher is familiar with the reader we are using. Nevertheless, e-books are going to grow fast and technology is likely to respond well.

E-Journals

Journals received in CD-format or on-line well in advance through electronic subscription is known as e-journals. Through this, the current and the back volumes are available in soft copy and on Internet. The full-text search across the titles and issues are available to users at desktops and the outputs can be viewed either at printed or e-mailed to other users.

The Electronic Publishing

The following major factors are responsible for the conservative publishers to accept the transition to publish e-journals:

(a) The convenience of web for access and browsing.

(b) The economics of Internet for delivery.

(c) The digital revolution which is promising instant delivery of complete information to user's desktop in a seamless manner.

Seamless access is a possibility through linking information resources like databases and e-journals distributed at several sites. With the onslaught of Internet and Intranet, the following three access models have emerged for e-journals:

(a) Remote access

(b) On site, at the library

(c) Access through databases.

Hazel Woodward and her colleagues of Loughborough University outlined the following myths about electronic journals:

1. Electronic journals are always more current than their print counterparts.
2. Electronic journals provide all graphic materials of their print counterparts.
3. Electronic journals are always accessible.
4. All readers have equal access to required computers at any time.
5. Electronic journals will save library staff time and effort in handling serials.

Mary Jean Pavelsek outlined a set of 11 "guidelines" for evaluating e-journals and their providers:

1. Economics
2. Ease of use and user flexibility
3. Archival implications
4. Future accessibility
5. Access
6. Licensing, copyright and distribution restrictions
7. Single or multiple publisher
8. Print vs. electronic comparisons
9. User support
10. If a package, is it "all or nothing"?
11. Planned enhancements.

E-Reports

The reports of any institution are scanned and converted to searchable portable document format (PDF). These reports are classified according to subject categories and archived in a server class machine and a detailed entry is made in a database for facilitating search. The reports with copyright are also digitized in the similar manner. These reports are published using the web technology and made accessible from user desktop. Title, keyword, report number, year and author can search these collections.

E-Database

E-Databases include heterogeneous CD-ROM based information resources, updating of CD-ROM collection, bibliographies and full text sources. These databases are web enabled, networked solutions or stand-alone CD-ROM solutions. Among those solutions the web enable from user desktops through the web browsers while the networked solution may require special installation mapping at the client side.

E-Content Pages

The idea behind e-content is to provide desktop access to the digitized content pages of books, conference proceedings, Journals, etc. This relieves the users from physical browse of the content pages of library documents and also reduces the damage done to them due to excessive physical browsing.

The textual information on the content pages can be processed using Optical Characters Recognizer (OCR) method in order to provide full search option on content pages of documents. This would facilitate the users to find topics or documents of their interest easily.

Many fill formats are available representing e-content pages like PDF, JPEG, GIF, TIF, etc. Among the above formats, the PDF is faster and economical for on-line viewing and archiving.

E-Clipping

The main objective of e-clippings is the retrospective search and comprehensive analysis of new items. It helps the users to retrieve new clips by simple clicks. The news items from different sources are identified and scanned at the earliest.

The routines for scanning and storing the clips, in other words the sources for the clips have to be made easy with suitable programs that would speed up the process. The news items are archived into server and users have the options to view them by specific data, duration, keyword or new source.

Advantages of E-Publishing and E-Journals

1. Electronic publishing is always more current than their print counterparts.
2. It provides graphic materials of their print counterparts and they are accessed easily.
3. E-publishing will save library staff time and effort in handling them.
4. Electronic publishing will bypass libraries and make them redundant.
5. Through electronic publishing, the storage and dissemination of information becomes inexpensive or free.
6. The fast and easy access to information is the major reason for the popularity of e-publishing. Search engines make it possible to retrieve the appropriate articles and most of the publishers provide keyword and author search thus reducing the role of additional indexing and abstracting. Electronic journals also provide hyperlink to cite related articles and other useful sources.
7. It facilitates better quality of service including value-added products, like electronic clipping service. User can set up profiles on most major databases to monitor customized news including current events, company and industry news, evolving issues and other topics of interest. Such an electronic clipping service provides professional news both in real-time and with periodic updates.

8. In electronic publishing, the data can be maintained up-to-date and this enables "on-demand publishing" and allows retrospective searching and SDI. The electronic version also provides Boolean search of the full text.
9. The most important advantage of EP over the conventional journal is the turnaround time in other words the time lag in submission, processing and dissemination of information. This ensures timely publication, which is of utmost importance to the research community.
10. It allows dual publishing in other words publishing of articles relevant to two different subjects in more than one journal.
11. It facilitates the user to see a "living article". In other words the user can log in at any time and see an experiment on an ongoing basis, showing data collected that day.
12. The electronic publishing has made it possible to publish material on an article-by-article basis, not bound to any specific weekly or monthly issue.
13. The user can access the relevant information without going to the library. The libraries can provide Internet connectivity and dial-up access to all its patrons so that they can access the subscribed databases and e-journals of the library from their home and workplace. This will facilitate the library and the information centers to cater to a more number of users and even geographically distributed users.
14. Other than the initial expenditure, the electronic publishing is cheaper than the conventional form of publishing and it is also environment friendly, as it does not require felling of trees for paper.

Conclusion

In the age of information, easy access to information is an essential prerequisite for the development of a country and access to information is also a hallmark of democracy. Hence, the developing countries like India should make earnest efforts to concentrate more on developing and using new electronic gadgets that provide better access to information. We have to make efforts to produce henceforth in digital form. This would reduce our expenditure in converting texts later to digital forms. Creating texts in digital form would facilitate in publishing of documents electronically either on the web or in the form of CDs, etc.

The universe of knowledge is expanding and its roots lie in the ever-growing corpus of information published through print and the electronic media. Electronic publishing is going to solve resource-sharing issues. However, it is going to do so, but it is going to happen in stages. The emerging information society would be required to combine the skills of traditional librarianship with those of a communicator, information analyst, web and net server. On this process, one should positively never forget those less privileged who cannot afford to pay for the 'Electronic Media' and for whom, the 'print media' in the form of traditional libraries still constitute a majority of population. In a pursuit for the electronic and digital excellence, libraries *vis-à-vis* information centers should have the ability and vision to co-exist with its traditional counterparts by cooperation, rapport, understanding, will power, determination and strong networking. If one could achieve this, our libraries and Information centers could easily stand up to the growing change and prepare itself to meet the challenges of the 'new millennium'.

Application of Library Network and the Role of Internet

14

Introduction

The term "Network" refers to a system of physically separate computers with telecommunication links through which they can exchange information and share resources. It is also used in the abstract sense to mean modes of interaction between people. It offers two services namely:

(i) Access to the people who use computers on the network by means of e-mail, conferencing or chat facilities.

(ii) It permits the use of files (text, graphics, audio and video), software, databases and peripherals (like printers or fax machine) stored on or attached to the computers on the network (LAN, WAN).

The wealth of information resources available on-line has given impetus to the idea of Electronic library.

Inter-Library Loan

A transaction involving the lending of library materials by one library to another is known as inter-library loan. The practice of inter-lending among library is based on a recognition that the resources of any one library are rarely if ever sufficient to meet all the needs of all its users. The introduction of computer paved the way for electronic databases out of groups of individual library catalogues and union catalogues transformed the inter-lending sense, by providing searches with millions of reference. OCLC (on-line computer library center) was the first U.S. based database originally created for cooperative cataloguing purpose started in 1979 for inter-lending by libraries both inside and outside the U.S.

Resource Sharing

Resource sharing has been considered as a powerful instrument for augmenting information sources in the context of 'distributed environment', and in the 'digital environment'. It is also an indispensable tool in the context of 'Information for all'. The collaborative, coordinated and cooperative endeavour aims at extending access to all the resources and services of the participating institutions, or information centers. The resource sharing in India has not been taken in full swing due to non-cooperative attitudes of librarians and insufficient funds.

Resource sharing denotes a mode of operation whereby functions are shared in common by a number of libraries. The goals are to provide a positive net effect:

(a) On the library user in terms of access to more materials or services;

(b) On the library budget in terms of providing level service at less cost, increased service at level cost, or much more service at less cost than if undertaken individually. These goals should be realized without harm to the missions of participating libraries, although their methods of operation invariably must be adjusted. Similarly, the goals are realizable only with some changes in the habits of users. The electronic network environment provides the following additional advantages for resource sharing among libraries and information centers:

- Instant communication among libraries facilities swift action for information exchange.
- It offers better means for acquisition and exchange of information and users satisfaction rate is much more than conventional ways of resource sharing.

(c) It makes no difference whether the participating library is five minutes drive or five thousand miles away. Networked environment therefore offers opportunities for libraries to participate at international level and work together for a common cause.

(d) Networked environment provides flexibility to help the users of participating libraries and try to do away with the procedure-oriented operations, rigid practices and strict codes of conduct:
   - Participating libraries having their Webpages, publicize their resources and services through such pages and hence facilitate motivation for joint action plans and programs among libraries for further development and improvement of library services.
   - It not only encourages more number of libraries to participate in the resource sharing programs, but also broadens the areas and scope of resource sharing.

In addition to the advantages of resource sharing through a networked environment, there are several opportunities like the networked libraries can develop their own intranet where a central information depositary can be planned which is developed and shared by all the participants over a period of time. The participating libraries' staff may use their information management abilities and skills to develop significant intranet, which may enhance their capabilities of providing comprehensive and timely library and information services to their clientele.

Agreements

There are several basic agreements among libraries that are important to develop, if a resource sharing system is to be achieved. The first agreement is to share currently owned materials with protocols, limitations and priorities carefully spelled out. The agreement should provide for an independent administration of resource sharing, but one, which does not emasculate the goals, and missions of the cooperation libraries. Funding should be based on an obligation for long-term support to permit the benefits to develop; the financial agreement should permit individual libraries to withdraw, but constrained to avoid disturbance of the system.

Second, there should be agreement on acquisitions policies, both to ensure consistent development of holdings and to avoid redundancy when this is judged jointly to be unproductive. Third, there should be agreement on bibliographic control, it would best if it is a standardization one so that users of each cooperating library may have a consistence means of accessing the catalogues of others. If standardization is not feasible, then the second best is the provision of adequate training for users and/or access to the local reference staff to provide aid in locating materials.

The other necessary agreements include definition of loan periods and renewals, procedures for earlier return of materials if needed, payment for lost materials, and other 'housekeeping' chores. The effectiveness of resource sharing depends on the availability of an infrastructure including appropriate communications, technology, and delivery systems. The computer has been an extremely effective device for processing and location materials quickly and conveniently regardless of distance, but again an adequate infrastructure must be assured consistent, reliable electric power, and appropriately trained personnel.

Need of Resource Sharing

1. Information explosion and scattering of literature both published and unpublished.
2. Difficulties experienced by library staff in handling enormous data.
3. Complexity and diversity of users' demands.
4. Constraints on libraries with regard to resources and facilities.
5. Ever increasing and ever changing nature of information and communication technologies and their impact on library and information services.
6. Emergence of electronic resources.
7. Diversified nature of bibliographic data storage facilities and practices.
8. Increasing cost of information materials and economic pressures.

9. Increasing emphasis on the optimum use of existing resources.
10. Increasing emphasis on eliminating unnecessary duplication of information sources.
11. Emergence of local, regional and national networks.
12. Emergence of interdisciplinary research and subject specialization.
13. The information-seeking pattern of varied users and the technological developments.

Goals of Resource Sharing

The resource sharing through networking is planned to achieve the following basic goals:

1. Computerized union database.
2. Shared catalogue service.
3. Maximize user satisfaction.
4. Minimizing cost and time in reaching the destination.
5. Shared circulation and inter-library loan services.
6. Shared database services such as abstracting, indexing and full text services.
7. Links with other automated library systems and services.

Barriers to Information Resource Sharing

1. Lack of infrastructure facilities available among the participating libraries.
2. Lack of awareness about the existing standards.
3. Provisions of copyright law.
4. Possessiveness among library personnel.
5. Lack of National Policy and established guidelines.

There are a number of constraints under which resource sharing networks must operate:

1. Delivery time for remotely accessed materials exceeds that for locally held materials.
2. Materials loaned are not available for local access.
3. Browsing among collections is inhibited.

4. If all libraries depend on the holdings of others there will be no substantial resources to share.
5. The sharing of resources may lead to institutions of fees by copyright holders.
6. An unfavourable 'balance of trade' may result in subsidy of non-local patrons.

It is obvious that resource sharing cannot be accomplished unilaterally; rather it requires concerted action of a number of libraries and entails changes in functions and attitudes on the part of users, librarians, and administrators. It typically entails the application of processes and technology, which exceeds the financial means of single libraries and probably requires involvement of nationally, supported activities.

Library Consortia

The term 'Consortia' refers to a cooperative arrangement among groups or institutions. In other words it is an association of libraries for some definite purpose. These libraries consortium is in the process of common subscription on consortium platform. The most beneficial properties of e-journals like round the clock accessibility, retrieval of information at light speed and mouse click access are the add on features. This may be summed up in the following manner:

(i) Sow less reap more by sharing the job.
(ii) Duplication may be avoided.
(iii) Professional manpower can be developed more efficiently.

For resource sharing among participatory library of consortium requires Union catalogue of books, journals, etc. They should be available on website.

Networking in India

Networks such as OCLC (on-line computer library center) and RLIN of the USA have been trendsetters in the area of resource sharing. Library Networks have been set up in India as well, the most prominent of them being DELNET, which was registered in 1992 as a society and currently has over 200 libraries as its members. Others being CALIBNET, MALIBNET the UGC has sponsored INFLIBNET in 1988, which is intended to emerge as a large network of universities, colleges and other academic libraries in the country.

INFLIBNET

Information and Library Network (INFLIBNET) is a major national effort to improve capability in information transfer and access, as support to scholarship, learning, research and academic pursuits. It would link up institutions of higher learning covering all disciplines. INFLIBNET was set up in 1993 by UGC to computerize and network the libraries of the universities and higher education institutes in India. It would be a multiple function/service network in the sense that it will also offer catalogue-based services, database services, document supply services, collection development and communication based services.

There would be a national center for managing, overseeing and coordinating the network administration and four regional centers which would maintain regional union catalogues apart form databases on projects, institutions and specialists. At the sectoral level. UGC's Information Centers and NISSAT Sectoral Centers or those performing national level functions/services in specific subjects/disciplines/missions would be included. End users will be served locally through college/Department/ University or R&D institutional centers.

The INFLIBNET is a project sponsored by the University Grants Commission of India to link the libraries and information centers including about 200 universities, over 7000 colleges, 400 Research and Development laboratories and other organizations. It is a computer network to put together all existing and anticipated information resources in a standard machine-readable form and to make it accessible to facilitate specific information search from almost any place in the country.

The INFLIBNET is a cooperative venture and realizes its success on cooperation of all its participants for mutual benefit. It is resource strength on its component, participants and their resource. This project is designed to library resource sharing by avoiding duplication in acquisition of library materials, to the extent possible. Resource sharing is the backbone activity of INFLIBNET. This programme promotes creation of conducive environment for library resource sharing through activities such as: identifying existing information sources, creating bibliographic databases, updating and maintaining the databases, making them accessible by providing interconnection and communication facilities, etc.

The major implications of INFLIBNET on resource sharing area:

- Creating awareness: The INFLIBNET through various regional, national meetings with librarians, vice-chancellors, teachers, etc. has created some awareness with respect to library resources, their sharing and networking.
- Accelerating Library Automation: Large number of libraries are computerizing their various library services. They are to extent possible, using the guidelines suggested by the INFLIBNET.

Networking of libraries and resource sharing will improve our services and increase the efficiency. INFLIBNET is for academic excellence; saving resources and equity. Resource sharing will provide many benefits to the academic and research community, which include access to large resources of information, precise and speedier dissemination of information and access to international information systems. In today's academic world, INFLIBNET have a significant role to play in National development. If we do not think of on-line resource sharing in a proper perspective right now, the condition of library services is bound to deteriorate in the year to come. However, in view of the fast changing information scenario, multifaceted development in IT; the time has now come for the development of coherent on-line resource sharing programme. This will not only solve most of the problems facing a university library, but will also help it to be more responsive to the needs of its users in the next millennium.

NISSAT

National Information System in Science and Technology (NISSAT) is on of the organs of Department of Science and Technology, Government of India. This agency is promoting libraries and information resources, networking and developing human skill in the field by financing networks, databases, seminars and conferences. NISSAT has encouraged interconnecting the libraries located at Delhi, Mumbai, Kolkata, Chennai, Hyderabad and Bangalore. The NISSAT programme envisages promotion and support to the development of a compatible set of information systems on science and technology interlinking them as a network. The approach adopted is to bring the existing centers, systems and services to a higher level of operations so that the interest of the national community of information users can be served.

CSIRNET

CSIR has set up a computer communication network (CSIRNET) for exchange of information among its 40 laboratories. The CSIRNET would help organize indigenous on-line database services on such subjects as leather technology, food technology, natural products, chemistry, radio physics and medicinal plants. It would provide bulletin board and set up teleconferencing facilities through the network apart from facilitating flow of routine administrative and financial information and exchange of library resources. Apart from accessing international databases through NACIDs, efforts are on way to develop databases on the expertise and sophisticated instruments available in various CSIR units, which would be of interest to users outside it also.

DRDONET

DRDONET is a proposed bibliographic information network for Defence, covering only unclassified scientific and technical information. The users of DRDONET would be scientific, research and defence personnel from the Department of Defence, Department of Defence R&D, and Department of Defence production and supplies. The defence bibliographic information network would also have close links with other similar networks like NICNET for exchange of information on mutually agreed terms. DESIDOC has taken the initiative in planning and implementing the DRDONET as a partially distributed network. There are more than 50 libraries under DRDO spread all over the country. DRDO network will have four regional databases located at Delhi, Pune, Hyderabad and Bangalore. All these regional databases will be networked in distributed database mode. The database building activities are almost complete. The network will become operational by the end of this year.

Institutions and Network in India

As many as 180 universities and over 6000 colleges use library services across the country for their academic and research activities and they depend on the resources available in their libraries. It is felt that the library network system alone would enable the universities and the higher learning institutes to function and serve its users well. The information sharing through computer networks and document delivery in the form of electronic media are helpful to the research scholars and the teaching faculties. Internet, the network of networks in the world referred to as the information superhighway, is growing at a very fast rate of 10 per cent every month, connected with more than 5,00,000 networks, interlinked with approximately a 2 million computer hosts having about 40 million users.

In India, the use of Internet has gained impetus through National Informatics Network (NICNET), which opened the floodgates of the Internet, and as a result, a drastic increase has happened in the number of Internet users. The Internet connectivity has become handy to access the electronic journals, bibliographic and full-text resources and to answer the reference questions.

Information infrastructure in India has not grown to the extent desirable. The Indian libraries have displayed a tendency to cling to conventional or traditional methods of dealing with bibliographic information even though the expertise to adopt and absorb modern information technology is not lacking in the country. There are many reasons which are inhibiting the development of digital and networking libraries in India:

1. Lack of adequate local and national infrastructure for handling information technology and networks.
2. Lack of well-trained workforce.
3. Non-availability of locally developed machine-readable documents.
4. Non-availability of well organized 'user nets' in different subjects both in public and private sectors.
5. Possible control and censorship of information by the local bodies, Governments or other entities.
6. Lack of freedom to access international electronic documents.

The functions of a library network can be broadly categorized into:

(i) Information services to users such as ILL access to databases, reference assistance, etc.

(ii) Support services to member libraries in technical processing, cooperative development programme.

(iii) Services for network administration such as evolution of network, training communication of activities through meetings, newsletters, etc.

To facilitate access to resources in the libraries in the network some measures have already been initiated and a few more are planned such as:

(i) Union list of current scientific serials in the libraries has already been compiled.

(ii) A directory of the libraries is the indication of the document delivery facilities also compiled.

(iii) Union catalogues of libraries that have the same sift ware and which are yet to start automation is being initiated.

India has developed national information and scientific networks as shown in the following chart:

NETWORK	Network used by	Controlled by
NICNET	Government departments and agencies	Planning Commission
ERNET	Institutions working in frontier areas of Science and Technology	Department of Electronics
CLAIBNET	Libraries in Kolkata	Under the auspices of NISSAT
DELNET	Libraries in Delhi	Under the auspices of NISSAT
BOMNET	Libraries in Mumbai	Under the auspices of NISSAT
MALIBNET	Libraries in Chennai	Under the auspices of NISSAT
HYDLIBNET	Libraries in Hyderabad	Under the auspices of NISSAT
BALNET	Libraries in Bangalore	Under the auspices of NISSAT
BTISNET	Academic and research biotechnology institutions	Department of Science and Technology
INFLIBNET	University libraries, college libraries and specialized R&D Institutions	UGC
SIRNET	Laboratories under the CSIR	CSIR

Future of Networks (Intellectual Property Right)

The universe of knowledge is expanding. The electronic publishing is going to solve resources sharing issues. To create a mechanism that facilitates the sharing of resources available in the participating libraries of a network. It is done by creating union catalogue of library resources, books, periodicals and articles, CDs, Videos and Theses. The gray literature in digital form and making them available to the participating libraries through on-line.

The products of human intellect are considered as personal property, especially protected by patents. The personal property may be divided into:

(i) Physical, tangible.

(ii) Intangible, incorporeal property, the intellectual property falls into the latter.

The copyright laws that are being violated due to digitization of information in many cases are at present under the process of amendment. The main issues that concern the digitized data are:

(a) Fair use appropriate preservation measures for long-term,

(b) Availability of digital publications.

The telecommunication laws and system have to ensure that intellectual property flows freely because of intellectual freedom and the laws and systems should not impose over to covert censorship on it. On the other the copyright laws provide due remuneration to publishers and others for their work transmitted digitally with protection of digital works. As a result, the US copyright office has lacked right of companies to limit access to their databases on the Internet and the agencies to protect all types of creative works on the web by introducing Internet Copyright Registration of works.

Conclusion

The shift in the libraries from the modern to the post-modern era reveals transformation taking place in various forms including the growth of virtual information resources and the use of multimedia applications. The modern libraries are expected to grow digital resources using international liability graphics standards and they are expected to publish all documents in digital form. In this digital era, the libraries need to join one or more library networks and share resources with other libraries.

Glossary of Technical Terms

1. Abstract

Abstract refers to a form of current bibliography in which sometimes books, but mainly contributions to periodicals, are summarised. They are usually accompanied by adequate bibliographical descriptions to enable the publications or articles to be traced and are arranged in classified order. They may be in the language of the original or be translated into English. In other words, it is a non-critical indication of the subject content of a document.

2. Academic Library

A library attached to a school or college or university is known as academic library. The main purpose of an academic library is to function as an auxiliary of the parent institution in carrying out its teaching programme effectively.

3. Accessioning

To register acquisitions of library materials, usually in the order in which they are added to a collection. Every volume added to the library receives a serial number in the order of acquisition to the library collection. This includes books purchased or received in exchange or as gift. This number is called accession number. Cumulated volumes of periodicals which are to be bound and preserved in the library, are also accessioned.

4. Access System

Libraries, where the users are allowed to consult the documents/reading materials freely without any physical barriers or any distinction is known as open access system. In some libraries where collection is of rare books, manuscripts, drawings, micrographic materials, closed access system is followed. In other words, users are not allowed into the stacks of these materials.

5. Acquisition

The processes of acquiring books for a library is known as acquisition. In other words, it is the process of identifying a desired item verifying a need, selecting a proper source and ordering. It includes in order follow-up, receiving and paying.

6. Added Entry

In cataloguing, it refers to a secondary entry, i.e. any entry other than main entry. It is the subsidiary entry under the joint authors, compiler, editor, translator, title, series or the subject of a book.

7. Administration

The library administration is responsible for the active management of a library, including the formation and carrying out the policies and plans. The administration of a library is the force behind the machinery of its working routine.

8. Analytical Entry

The analytical entry is the entry of some part of a book, or of some articles contained in some collection, volumes of essays, serials, etc., including a reference to the publication which contains the article or work entered. This entry is supplementary to the comprehensive or main entry for the whole work. The entries may be made under authors, subjects or titles.

9. Anglo-American Cataloguing Rules (AACR)

There are two types of catalogues, namely, classified catalogue and dictionary catalogue and there are two catalogue code books which support each type of the catalogue. They are:

1. Classified Catalogue Code (CCC)
2. Anglo-American Cataloguing Rules (AACR)

The AACR-1 and 2 were published in 1967 and 1978 respectively by the American Library Association, the Canadian

Library Association, the Library of Congress and the British Library Association.

10. Automation

The technology concerned with the design and development of progress and systems that minimise the necessity of human intervention in their operation. In the context of library, the automation is the mechanisation or computerisation of all library operations.

11. Bibliography

A bibliography is a printed list of documents containing formal descriptions of the documents. In other words, it is a list of books and sometimes of other materials such as periodical articles and illustrations, written by one author or on one subject, arranged according to some permanent principle.

12. Book Number

A combination of letters and figures assigned to a book in order to distinguish it from all other books in the same class. In colon classification, it follows the class number and precedes the collection number to form the call number. It is the symbol used to fix the position of a book in relation to other books having the same ultimate class.

13. Browne System

In this, the borrower's ticket bears a pocket to hold the book card of the book issued out. The borrower's ticket bears the details of the user—name, membership number and address. When a reader wishes to borrow a book, the staff removes the book card from the book and inserts it in the borrower's card and keeps the same in the charging tray to be filed.

14. Budget

Budget is the total amount of money which is available for library purposes after the estimate of anticipated needs has been approved by the appropriate authority. Thus a library budget is an annual estimate of expected income and expenditure of the library for the coming year.

15. Call Number

It is the number or combination of figures and letters which indicate location of the book on the shelves. It consists of collection number, the class number and the book number. The class number fixes the position of a book's specific subject relative to other subjects.

16. Catalogue

It is a list of books which is arranged on a definite plan. It is the list of holdings of a library. It is an ordered compilation of bibliographic descriptions and sufficient information to afford access to the documents available in a library.

17. Centralised Cataloguing

It is the cataloguing of all books in a library system at one central point, i.e. books are not catalogued at the individual libraries to which they are allocated. In other words, it is the cataloguing by one library or cataloguing office within a system of libraries, of all books acquired by all those libraries so that the results of such cataloguing are used by the individual libraries.

18. Chain Procedure

It is a method of constructing subject index entries, without permutation of components by citing terms contained in particular chains. It is the standardised procedure whereby the successive terms in a chain of classes are transformed into heading for an alphabetical index.

19. Charging

In case a user wants to borrow a book from the library, he goes to the counter where the circulation staff issues the book to him. This activity is known as charging of books (issuing).

20. Circulation Section

It is one of the important sections in a library. The circulation section is involved in the activities such as charging and discharging of books, overdue collection, maintaining statistics and enrolling new members to the library. In other words, here the books are circulated to the readers.

21. Classification

The library classification is a process of putting books and other reading material on a subject in a logical sequence on the shelves which could be helpful to the users. The classification is one of the most important steps in the organization of libraries and has been rightly called the foundation of librarianship.

22. Classified Catalogue

It is a catalogue in which an entry is made under the class mark which represents the book's subject in the classification scheme chosen. Arrangement follows the order of the classification scheme. In other words, it is a catalogue of subject entries which are arranged in systematic order according to a scheme of classification. It has two parts, viz., the alphabetical and classified part.

23. Classified Catalogue Code

It is a catalogue code consisting of a set of specific rules which are used in building up uniform and consistent entries for a collection. It simplifies the task of the cataloguers and is a great boon to the users. Two important catalogue codes are: 'Classified Catalogue Code' of Dr. S.R. Ranganathan and the 'Anglo-American Cataloguing Rules' (AACR). The CCC of Ranganthan provides rules for entries in a catalogue.

24. Cooperative Cataloguing

It is the cataloguing of books and the distribution of cards or slips by a central agency, e.g. the Library of Congress in the USA and the BNB in the UK. In other words, it is the sharing of common cataloguing operations by a number of libraries to avoid the duplication of effort.

25. Cross Reference

It is a reference from one heading to another. In other words, cross reference refers to the host document wherein the subject has appeared as a fragment and not as a whole. It is a direction in a catalogue, from one of several headings under which an entry might be sought, to the heading adopted, or to draw attention to other headings under which related material gets entered, e.g. AVES see BIRDS.

26. Current Awareness Service (CAS)

It is a service which provides users with the latest information, or published literature, on their particular subject interest to keep abreast of the current trends in their respective fields. The list of current additions to the library also serves the purpose of CAS.

27. Descriptive Cataloguing

The descriptive cataloguing refers to the part of the cataloguing process which is concerned with the choice and form of main and added entries, transcription of title—page details, collation, etc.

28. Dictionary Catalogue

It is a catalogue that arranges its entries and references in a single alphabet like a dictionary. In other words, it is a catalogue of entries under authors, editors, translators, title, subjects, form and series which together with the necessary references are arranged in general alphabetical sequence.

29. Discharging

As explained in 'charging', discharging refers to return of books by the readers at the circulation section. The work relating to return of books is referred to as discharging work.

30. Dissemination

It refers to the supply of information or records from a storage point to persons or organizations. It is one of the functions of a library. The others are collection (acquisition), storing, processing and the last function is to disseminate the information gathered (to supply or distribute).

31. Documentation

Documentation refers to the act of collecting, classifying and making readily accessible the records of all kinds of intellectual activity. It also refers to the science of collecting, storing and organising recorded informational materials or documents for optimum uses. The documentation services include abstracting, indexing, translation, photocopying and compilation of bibliographies.

32. Document Explosion

As a result of invention of printing press and industrial revolution, the book production is increasing in leaps and bounds. The document explosion is the direct outcome of knowledge explosion. The librarians of today have a tough time in managing both the increase of documents and users. Books and other reading materials are produced voluminously as a result of knowledge explosion.

33. Entry

The recording of a book in a catalogue under a suitable heading, is known as an entry. There are two entries in a catalogue namely, main entry and added entry.

34. Extension Service

The extension service is the supplying of books and other library assistance to individuals or organizations outside a library's regular service area. The extension services include the book exhibition, lectures on current topics, arranging film shows and cultural programmes. It is well organised in public libraries.

35. Facet

The term 'facet' is a technical term, meaning an 'aspect', 'dimension' or 'a characteristic'. A facet is the total of sub-classes got by dividing a subject into sub-classes on the basis of one aspect or characteristic. In other words, facet is an aspect under which a group of concepts may be looked at to have something general in common.

36. Fundamental Categories

It was Ranganathan who introduced the idea of 'Fundamental Category'. It is a root concept to which a facet "is related explicitly or implicitly". To him there are five fundamental categories, which are: Personality, Matter, Energy, Space and Time.

37. House-keeping Operations

Activities related to acquisition of books, classification, cataloguing, book circulation and book maintenance are traditionally known as house-keeping operations.

38. Indexing

It is a method which is used to retrieve information from a table in memory or a file on a direct access store. An index is known as an ordered reference list of the contents of a file or document together with references for identification or location of those contents.

39. Information

Information means, 'facts being communicated' and it is a 'message' used to represent a fact or concept by the unity of a data medium and its meaning. Thus an information is a data, or a fact or knowledge. It is the product of human brain in action.

40. Information Retrieval

Information retrieval is the action of or methods and procedures for recovering specific information from a collection of stored data. It is a method of finding documents, or the information contained in documents, in a library or other collection, selectively recalling recorded information. Classification, indexing and machine searching through computers have been the other systems of information retrieval. It concerns with the techniques and processes of representation, storage, organization and accessioning of information.

41. Information Technology

'IT' may be defined as a combination of computer and telecommunications techniques which makes possible new systems and products to help people. Thus 'IT' is the application of a wide variety of electronic technologies such as computer, telecommunications, micrographic, reprographics, video recording, etc. for the storage, retrieval, reproduction and dissemination of information in the library environment.

42. ISBD

In order to create and maintain international standards in bibliographic descriptions for easy flow of information, IFLA started the programme of the International Standard Bibliographic Description (ISBD) to be applied by national bibliographies and other information sources. It can be converted into machine-readable form.

43. ISBN

The International Standard Book Number is an internationally standardised number assigned to books by the publishing houses for reference.

44. ISSN

The International Standard Serial Number is an internationally standardised number assigned to serials/journals for reference. It is used for identification, ordering and processing of serial publications. It also facilitates computerisation of serials catalogue records by providing machine-readable serials records.

45. Inter-Library Loan

Inter-library loan is a cooperative arrangement among libraries by which one library may borrow materials from another library. It is one of the principles of resource sharing project.

46. Inventory System

See Stock Verification (78).

47. Knowledge Explosion

See Document Explosion (32).

48. Laws of Library Science

Dr. S.R. Ranganathan, the father of Library Science in India, formulated the five laws of library science in 1923. According to him these laws are the fundamental laws of library science. The essence of these laws are that books are meant for use and user is the prime factor and his time must be saved:

1. Books are for use
2. Every reader has his/her book
3. Every book has its reader
4. Save the time of the reader
5. Library is a growing organism.

49. Library Committee

It is the government of a library. It refers to the committee which is responsible for the provision of library budget and service. In other words, the library committee is a body or an organization consisting of persons being assigned a particular job.

50. Library Legislation

Library legislation is very important for the establishment, development and maintenance of public libraries in any state. To provide better services to readers, the library requires huge money. It is the legislation of government through its library cess fund that provides facilities to the public libraries. It was by the tireless efforts of Ranganathan that the Madras Library Act came into force.

51. Library Organization

Organization can be defined as an 'organised body'. It is an aggregation of individuals. It is the act or process of organising, i.e. creating a systematic work together for a common end. In other words, the organization creates the machine, the administration runs it.

52. Library Science

It is the branch of learning concerned with collecting, storing and distributing written or printed records by means of libraries and also with the management of libraries.

53. Library Statistics

It refers to the statistics maintained at the counter. It includes the number of visitors, number of books issued and returned. The most important advantage of maintaining statistics is that they are of immense value for the preparation of the annual report. They also help in preparing the budget estimates for the next financial year.

54. Long Range Reference Service

See Reference Service (71).

55. MARC

An acronym derived from the phrase Machine-Readable Cataloguing. This is a term referring to bibliographic information that has been encoded and transcribed into a machine-readable form to permit its manipulation—processing, transmission, etc. using the technology of Electronic Data Processing (EDP).

56. Main Entry

The principle entry of a book usually contains the fullest particulars. As a rule, the main entry is the author entry. It is the entry normally under the author of a book or where the author is not known, under the title and in some cases under the editor or the compiler of a work.

57. Maintenance Section

It refers to the section where the staff is engaged in weeding out unused books, sending worn-out books for binding and the preservation of books from pests. Besides, it undertakes the task of dusting and cleaning of book racks.

58. Management

The term management is defined as the process of planning, organising, leading and controlling the efforts of organizational members and the use of other organizational resources in order to achieve the desired goal. In other words, the management can be considered as a process which involves both art and science. The major functions of management are planning, organising directly, co-ordinating and budgeting.

59. Microform

It refers to any miniature form containing 'micro-images'. Microforms are the minute reproductions of documents, either produced photographically as microfilm or microcard, or by offset printing as microprints. It considerably reduces the pressure on storage space. It includes microfilm, microfiche, microcard, microprints, etc.

60. Monograph

It is a systematic and complete treatise on a particular subject, usually detailed in treatment but not extensive in scope. It need not be bibliographically independent.

61. National Library

It is the library which is responsible for acquiring and conserving copies of all significant publications published in the country. It may function as a 'legal deposit library'. It is responsible for producing a national bibliography. The National

Library, Kolkata is responsible for producing Indian National Bibliography.

62. Network

It refers to a complex arrangement of inter-connected elements. Through the network system, the resource sharing is practiced. The information technology has paved the way for computer networking system where the information can be exchanged without any delay of time.

63. Network System

It is a method of recording book loans which is most widely used in America. Each borrower has a ticket or card with spaces for recording loans. In this system, while issuing a book, the circulation assistant withdraws the book card from the book and notes down the registration number of the borrower and puts due date on the book card, date slip and the borrower's card, then returns the book and the borrower's card.

64. On-Line

An on-line system is one in which both the programme and data is directly entered into a computer and output directly transmitted to a device or location wherever it may be. Further in an on-line system, one can interact with the system effectively.

65. Organization

See Library Organization (51).

66. POSDCORB

Gulick and Urwick coined an acronym for the functions of management as 'POSDCORB' which stands for the following seven functions:

Planning, Organising, Staffing, Directing, Co-ordinating, Reporting and Budgeting.

67. Preservation

Book preservation is carried out in the maintenance section. In involves sending damaged books for binding, converting the important books into micro form, fumigation services and dusting and cleaning services. Besides, the books have to be preserved from insects, rodents, light, heat, moisture, fire and human-beings.

68. Primary Sources

Primary sources refer to the fundamental authoritative material relating to a subject used in the preparation of other written work. They are original manuscripts, contemporary records or documents which are used by an author in writing a book or other literary compilation.

69. Pseudonym

A name used by an author, which is not his real name. It is also known as 'pen name'.

70. Public Library

It is a 'library' which serves the population of a community or region free of charge or for a nominal fee. It refers to a library which is approved wholly or partly from public funds, and the use of which is not restricted to any class of persons in the community and is freely available to all.

71. Reference Service

It refers to the provision and organization of reference work by a library. It is the personalised assistance rendered by the library staff to the users in finding an information in connection with their study and research. It is rendered directly and personally and it is also known as 'information service' in modern context. There are two types of reference services, viz., ready reference service and long range reference service. The ready reference service is done by supplying annual reports, encyclopaedias, directories, etc. The long range service is done by getting information from other libraries. It involves certain amount of time.

72. Resource Sharing

No library is independent, since it cannot get all the materials its readers like. Hence the library, through this system, exchanges resources among the participating libraries.

73. Secondary Sources

Secondary sources of information are those which are either compiled from or refer to primary sources of information. These contain information regarding primary or original information, e.g. periodicals, indexes, encyclopaedias, etc.

74. Selective Dissemination of Information (SDI)

It is a service which continually disseminates documents, references, 'abstracts' or data selected according to the interest profiles of the users. It is one of the specialised modern information services.

75. Series Entry

It is an 'entry' in a catalogue of the several works which belong to a series under the name of the series as a heading.

76. Short Range

See Reference Service (71).

77. Specialised Library

It refers to the library which is organised to serve the needs of specialist readers of different kinds. In a special library, the readers are restricted in quality and number. The reading materials too are restricted in subject coverage, standard and number. The mode of service also is specialised in its nature.

78. Stock Verification

It is one of the important functions of a library. It is a general fact that books are misplaced in an open access system. Hence, it is the duty of the staff to go in for stock verification and shelf-rectification. All the books acquired by the library can be accounted for. Stock verification means a physical check-up of the documents on record.

79. Subject Catalogue

It is a 'catalogue' consisting of subject entry only. It refers to any catalogue which is arranged by subjects, whether in alphabetical or classified order, which directs users to the documents required by them.

80. Subject Entry

It is an 'entry' of a document in a file under a heading which indicates the subject of the document. In other words, it is an entry under the name of the specific subject treated by the book.

In CCC the number entry, 'the call number'—is the subject entry, since the call number is assigned according to the subject.

81. Technical Section

It refers to the section where the technical works like classification and cataloguing are done.

82. Tertiary Sources

Tertiary sources of information contain distilled information collected from primary and secondary sources. The aim of this source is to aid the searcher of information in the use of primary and secondary sources of information.

83. Tracing Section

It is the indication on the main card of all added entries and reference. This is done on the back of the card. Tracing is especially necessary in a dictionary catalogue.

84. Union Catalogue

It refers to the common 'catalogue' of the collections of several libraries. A union catalogue is a comprehensive catalogue of two or more libraries for the benefit of their users. In other words, it is a catalogue showing location of all the books in the libraries of an organised area.

85. University Library

It is a library or group of libraries established, maintained, and administered by a university to meet the needs of its students and members of the academic staff.

Bibliography

Bose, H., *Information Science, Principles and Practice*, New Delhi, Sterling Publishers, 1986.

Brophy, Peter, *Library in the Twenty-first Century*, London, Library Association Publishing, 2001.

Chopra, R.N., *Dictionary of Library Science*, New Delhi, Anmol Publications, 1990.

Dutta, D.N., *Introduction to Library Cataloguing*, Calcutta, The World Press, 1980.

Feather, John and Paul Sturges, *International Encyclopedia of Information and Library Science*, London, Routledge, 1997.

Kaul, H.K., *Library and Information Networking*, New Delhi, Delnet, 2000.

Kumar, Krishan, *Library Manual*, New Delhi, Vikas Publishing House, 1984.

——, *Reference Service*, New Delhi, Vikas Publishing House, 1984.

Kumar, P.S.G., *Computerization of Indian Libraries*, New Delhi, B.R. Publishing Corporation, 1987.

——, *Fundamentals of Information Science*, New Delhi, S. Chand & Co., 1998.

Malwad, N.M. et al., *Digital Libraries: Dynamic Storehouse of Digitized Information*, New Delhi, New Age International, 1996.

Misra, Jogesh, *History of Libraries and Librarianship in Modern India Since 1850.*

Muhammad Riaz, *Library Automation*, New Delhi, Atlantic Publishers (P) Ltd., 1992.

National Conference on Recent Advances in Information Technology; on Digital Asset Management, Chennai, IIT, 2001.

Navalani, K. and N.N. Gidwani, *Practical Guide to Colon Classification*, New Delhi, Oxford IBM, 1981.

Ohdeadar, A.K. and B. Sengupta, *Library Classification*, Calcutta, The World Press, 1977.

Rajagopalan, A., *Libraries of the Digital Age*, New Delhi, SBS Publishers and Distributors Pvt. Ltd., 2006.

Ravindra Rao, K., *Library Automation*, New Delhi, Wiley Eastern, 1992.

Satija, M.P., *Manual of Practical Colon Classification*, New Delhi, Sterling Publishers, 1984.

Sharma, C.D., *Use of Libraries*, New Delhi, Metropolitan, 1977.

Sharma, J.S., *Fundamentals of Library Science*, Chennai, Macmillan, 1977.

——, *Library Organization*, New Delhi, Vikas Publication, 1978.

Sharma, Ram Saroop, *Bibliography and Documentation*, Patiala, Madam Publishers, 1974.

Wersig, Gernot and Ulrich Neveling, *Terminology of Documentation*, Paris, UNESCO, 1975.